PICTURES IN THE AIR

The Story of the
National Theatre of the Deaf

PICTURES IN THE AIR

The Story of the
National Theatre of the Deaf

STEPHEN C. BALDWIN

Gallaudet University Press
Washington, D.C.

Gallaudet University Press
Washington, DC 20002

*Library of Congress Cataloging-in-
Publication Data*

Baldwin, Stephen C., 1944–
    Pictures in the air : the story of
the National Theatre of the Deaf /
Stephen C. Baldwin.
        p.   cm.
    Includes bibliographical refer-
ences and index.
    ISBN 1-56368-025-4 (acid-free) :
24.95
    1. National Theatre of the
Deaf—History. 2. Deaf, Theater
for the—History. I. Title.
HV2508.B35   1993
792'.087'2—dc20   93-37250
                              CIP

Posters in chapter opening
photos courtesy of NTD

For Oscar G. Brockett, my mentor

CONTENTS

Appendixes

FOREWORD

*O*n the fall of 1978, I met a scenic and lighting designer named Bob Steinberg through a mutual friend, J Ranelli. J was directing a play of mine in New York.

Bob and I discovered right off that we shared one huge—I'm talking large—mutual love: Mel Brooks and Carl Reiner's "Two Thousand Year Old Man." Both of us can quote the entire record; together we can assume either, or if one of us is tired, both parts.

I remember J telling me that Bob was married to a deaf woman who was an actor with some theater company I'd never heard of and the name of which I had a hard time keeping straight. Is it the National Theatre *for* the Deaf or the National *of* the Deaf. I know the two words connote a big distinction, I just don't happen to remember which is the right one.

Whatever the proper name of the company, I knew that J directed for them, but consumed with the delirium of doing a new play with a new director, I really didn't inquire about what he did with them or who they were.

That winter, J and I workshopped another play of mine, this time at the University of Rhode Island, where J and Bob were on the faculty. One evening, in the farmhouse to which I am told she had "retired" to raise her two sons, I met Bob's wife.

Her name is Phyllis Frelich and we changed each other's lives.

At the time I met Phyllis, I had no deaf or hard of hearing people in my family and none among my friends, students, or acquaintances (some who didn't listen, to be sure, but none who couldn't hear). I had no knowledge of deaf culture or American Sign Language or of any of the battles raging among those who would tell deaf people how to become educated or how to become part of the "real" world—the hearing world. The closest I had come to any experience with the deaf world, really, is through William Gibson's stunning play, *The Miracle Worker.*

The evening I met Phyllis Frelich, she told me that she was a founding member of the National Theatre *of* the Deaf, but that she had grown weary of the roles available to her with NTD and so had retreated here to this tiny farm. She wished, she said, that there were roles in "the hearing theater" for deaf actors.

Well, two things occurred to me: I had been told by J Ranelli, whom I trust, that Phyllis Frelich is not just a good actor, but an extraordinary one; and I was imbued with a fair amount of ego. So, I told Phyllis Frelich that I would write a role for her.

After I left, she and Bob confided later, they thought, "We've heard that before; he won't do it."

The following spring I became head of the theatre arts department at New Mexico State University. I called Phyllis and Bob and invited them to come teach and work with me for a semester beginning in January of 1979. At that time, I told them, I would have a play, with a role for Phyllis, ready to workshop.

Children of a Lesser God, the result of our collaboration, is one of the most satisfying and educational experiences any of us could ever have dreamed might be available in this difficult world.

Several years later, at an audition for the Dallas Theater Center production of *Children* (which I directed for my friend and mentor, Paul Baker) I met a young teacher and aspiring play-wright and actor named Steve Baldwin who had written to me some months before to tell me that, given the chance, he thought he could play my hard of hearing rebel, Orin Dennis.

And indeed, after the audition, I cast Steve in the role. I told him I wanted to find some deaf talent to use in the production, either as the main actors or understudies. Steve arranged for me to visit SouthWest Collegiate Institute for the Deaf in Big Spring, Texas, and I was deeply touched to be met there by students and faculty as someone who is a friend of the deaf.

From this school I took two actors, Cliff Bodiford, to under-study Steve, and Marilyn Myers, to understudy Bobbie Beth Scoggins, the young woman I was fortunate to find in Dallas to play Sarah.

Bobbie Beth later became a member of NTD, earned a doc-torate, and became a powerful advocate for deaf culture and rights. Steve Baldwin went on to get his Ph.D. in theatre from the University of Texas at Austin and, among other works, to write this book.

I think it's fair to say Steve and I were friends from the mo-ment we met at those auditions in Dallas, and that the friendship cemented through the crucible of building the Dallas Theater Center production of *Children of a Lesser God* and continued through Steve's ferocious drive to finish his Ph.D., a decade-long process during which we periodically shared our thoughts on everything from the lunacy of prejudice to the joys of exer-cise and fatherhood.

Despite my friendship with Steve, despite my outsider's inside relationship to the deaf world, I feel a little peculiar, in this era of rigid and often mind-boggling political correctness, writing the introduction to a book by a deaf writer about an extraordinary institution I knew far too little about until I read his book.

I'm embarrassed to confess that I did not see NTD perform until 1989, when my department invited the company to perform at NMSU. The production, *The King of Hearts,* ironically enough, had been brilliantly adapted and directed by J Ranelli.

Though I was ignorant until Steve Baldwin's book enlightened me to the history of NTD, it's fair to say the National Theatre of the Deaf provided me with scores of NTD alumni collaborators, in addition to Phyllis, Bob, and J, who have affected my life in large and small ways. Over the decade and a half that leads from that night in Rhode Island in 1978 when I met Phyllis Frelich to the Tony Awards in New York to the road companies and the scores of productions all over the country of *Children of a Lesser God,* I have been fortunate to work with some of the talents mentioned in this book; people such as Lewis Merkin, Linda Bove, Freda Norman, Julianna Fjeld, Richard Kendall, Lou Fant, Ed Waterstreet, Howie Seago, Rita Corey, Fred Voelpel, Janice Cole, and Bob Daniels—to name only those with whom I have spent hours and days at fruitful harvest.

Ultimately, of course, I am honored by Steve's request, for our friendship crosses cultures and speaks of the effort on both our parts to understand one another and to become as unified in our humanity as possible.

This, of course, is what NTD does so exceptionally well: It reaches out, it crosses boundaries, it brings disparate cultures together and shows us not only how we are unique but what we share. Would that more institutions that claim to do such things actually did.

I am also happy to be able to say how much I enjoyed reading *Pictures in the Air,* my friend's book, because I know how long and hard he worked to write it. I am as grateful for the honor of writing these words as I am for the cure of my ignorance.

MARK MEDOFF
Las Cruces, New Mexico

PREFACE

lthough the National Theatre of the Deaf (NTD) has achieved national and international recognition, relatively little historical information is readily available about it. The purpose of this book is to remedy that lack by presenting a comprehensive look at the development of NTD from 1959 to 1993, from the time certain individuals and groups joined forces to create a fully professional acting company of deaf artists in 1967 to its current hard-earned fame.

In telling the story of NTD, I have made use of previous studies, only two of which have been published. Helen Powers's book, *Signs of Silence* (1972), is a biography of Bernard Bragg, an NTD founding member. The book includes significant historical information on the early years of NTD. Bernard Bragg wrote his autobiography, *Lessons in Laughter,* which was translated by Eugene Bergman, in 1989. The book provides an interesting anecdotal perspective of NTD.

Four other studies of NTD have been written but not published. George McClendon's "The Unique Contribution of the National Theatre of the Deaf to the American Stage" (Master's thesis, Catholic University, 1972) draws considerably on information supplied by the late Sam Edwards, a former NTD member. McClendon's study, now twenty-one years old, was written too early to assess the importance of NTD. The late Dorothy Miles, a talented deaf actress, wrote her thesis, "A History of Theatre Activities in the Deaf Community of the U.S." (Master's thesis, Connecticut College) in 1974. Miles's work contains valuable information about the deaf American stage and is particularly important because she had been an NTD company member for four years, knew the deaf community well, and wrote from a deaf perspective. The third thesis, "The Theatre of the Deaf in America: The Silent Stage" (Master's thesis, Southern Illinois, 1979), was written by John Heidger. Heidger's primary method of research involved interviewing people, and most of the people he talked to were hearing. Nancy Bowen Tadie's dissertation, "A History of Drama at Gallaudet College: 1864 to 1969" (New York University, 1978), also proved to be an important source of information.

While all six of these studies contain important information, none presents a comprehensive picture of NTD. Hence, the challenge for me to pursue my personal mission in life.

When I visited NTD for the first time in 1978, I started to collect information, take pictures, and keep in touch with NTD. When Jack Gannon's inspiring book, *Deaf Heritage: A Narrative History of Deaf America* (1981) first came out, I seriously decided to pursue my goal to write about NTD. I finished the first manuscript in 1989, but had to spend three more years revising it. In the meantime, I continued to collect pictures and other historical materials to update the book. The results of my work are now contained within the covers of this book. Frankly, I am glad I waited fifteen years to complete this mission.

ACKNOWLEDGMENTS

*M*any people deserve more than hand waves of sincere applause for their role in making this book possible. Oscar G. Brockett, to whom this book is dedicated, taught me well in the history of theater, theory, and criticism at the University of Texas at Austin, where I earned my doctorate. Carol Hart Perry provided valuable assistance in typing several drafts of the original manuscript. Then along came Paula Bartone-Bonillas who edited and typed two critical revisions of the manuscript. Shanny Mow, my most faithful colleague, was there when I needed him the most. He critiqued the manuscript with extreme care. Jack Gannon also proved to be a valuable reader, critic, and supporter.

I sincerely appreciate the cooperation of David Hays, Laine Dyer, and other members of NTD from the time I started to develop the book in 1978. Ivey Pittle Wallace, the managing editor at Gallaudet University Press, taught me why patience and perseverance should go hand-in-hand. I thank her and the Gallaudet University Press staff for their work and cooperation. I also appreciate the efforts of Dr. Mary Hoyle, Laurence L. Baldwin, Joanne Cope Powell, and Marvin Sallop and the Texas School for the Deaf. And last, but certainly not least, my heartfelt thanks to all the people who believed in my mission to write the story of the National Theatre of the Deaf.

PICTURES IN THE AIR

The Story of the
National Theatre of the Deaf

PROLOGUE

*I*n 1959 you could buy a six-pack of Coke at the corner grocery store for a quarter. Stylish Studebakers and Hudsons rolled down city streets. A gallon of gasoline could be gotten for sixteen cents. Marilyn Monroe reigned. Elvis had released another hit, and Eisenhower was president.

The dawn of a new era was upon us.

Space flight was about to become a reality. Martin Luther King was gaining momentum, marching solidly forward with a civil rights movement that would have strong implications for all minority groups. America was soon to undergo dramatic social change.

Black theater was beginning to win commercial attention. *A Raisin in the Sun,* the first significant play written by a black playwright (Lorraine Hansberry), had won the New York Drama Critics Circle Best Play of the Year Award. This play, a penetrating drama about a black family's life, proved to be a major step forward for minority theater professionals. Not only was it written by a black woman, a black director (Lloyd Richards) directed a primarily black cast that included Sidney Poitier and Lou Gossett, Jr., in the play that took Broadway by storm in 1959.

The stage was being set for changes in deaf theater.

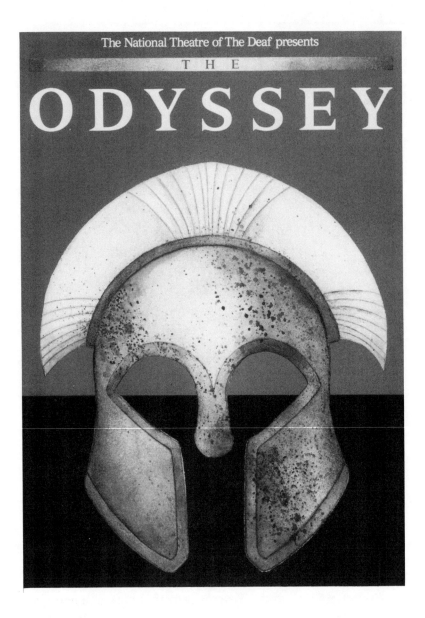

CHAPTER 1

Setting the Stage

rior to the birth of the National Theatre of the Deaf, deaf theater in America primarily meant weekend skits, mime shows, and signed songs or poems. Until 1967, in order to see "deaf theater," one attended the local deaf club, which was typically a rented hall just outside of the hubbub of downtown activity.

On Saturday nights, the local members gathered, joining to participate in bingo games, captioned film showings, regular meetings, cultural events, and the warm camaraderie so often found in minority groups sharing strong cultural bonds.

Most of the clubs sported an assortment of athletic trophies and plaques, proudly displaying their members' athletic prowess. Countless flyers and messages posted haphazardly along another wall kept everyone updated on the latest social or athletic activities. A bar, lined with an array of liquor and spirits, filled one side of the huge room. The blare of the jukebox reverberated throughout the club, where flying hands took little notice of the music. Some played poker; others pool. Blue-collar workers were by far the majority, and all looked forward to the solace they gained from the close-knit fellowship of their deaf comrades.

One blank wall with a raised platform in front was reserved for entertainment. The performances, usually impromptu, were mostly repeats of the mime shows and skits the group had seen countless times before. To signal the beginning of a show, hall lights were flashed on and off, commanding the attention of the members.

A lone mime comes onto the platform and does a Charlie Chaplin act, a reminder of the golden days of the silent movies when the deaf community enjoyed the same entertainment as their hearing counterparts. Many of the elderly deaf club members cursed the advent of the "talkie movies" and "talkie radios," the entertainment forms that had forced them into further isolation. The mime performs another favorite: a cowboy routine where he skillfully uses two fingers of each hand to suggest a mustache, guns, hats, or horse's mane. His creative use of fingers, hands, arms, legs, and most of all, his expressive face, mesmerizes his growing audience. Little by little, poker games, gossip, pool, and even the jukebox cease. The hall lights remain bright and the members focused as the mime performs his last routine, though many have seen it a hundred times before.

In addition to the amateurish performances found in some of the deaf clubs, literary societies at state residential schools for the deaf often presented long one-act plays as well as sign-singing, poetry presentations, and some dancing. No one ever dreamed of making acting a professional career.

In New York City, there were three major, sometimes overlapping, deaf grass-roots theater groups. The Metropolitan Theatre Guild of the Deaf was established in 1957 by Richard Myers and Joe Hines.[1] Another group, the New York Hebrew Association of the Deaf, saw many productions staged and acted by noted deaf actor-manager Wolf Bragg.[2] For many years, Bragg was also part of the third group, the New York Theatre Guild of the Deaf.

These three amateur deaf theater groups usually performed short original skits, mime shows, poetry, or sing-song programs, but no full-length productions. There were other groups in Washington, D.C., Chicago, and San Francisco.

These groups utilized natural talent and genuine American Sign Language. They performed infrequently, and rarely used interpreters or performed before the nonsigning public. Their primary goal was to entertain the deaf community and affirm deaf culture.

While talented performers could be found in deaf communities across the country, until Gallaudet University started formal drama classes in 1961, there were no college-level programs or theaters for aspiring actors who were deaf. Deaf theater, however, was about to enter a new era.

On Broadway, a relatively unknown actress—Anne Bancroft—was preparing for her stage role as Annie Sullivan in William Gibson's *The Miracle Worker,* a play adapted from the 1957 television production of the same name. At the time, Bancroft had little following in Hollywood. Having made a string of undistinguished movies, she had attracted little attention from critics or producers. Discouraged, she had returned to New York to the stage. There, she found success, first appearing in *Two for the Seesaw,* also written by William Gibson and directed by Arthur Penn. Her next role would be that of Annie Sullivan, once again teamed with Gibson and Penn.

Bancroft absorbs her characters, as would be demonstrated time and again in the years to come. The role of Annie would be complex and demanding: to "become" the woman who would connect an incorrigible deaf, blind, and mute child to her world would take a deep, empathic understanding of deafness.

So that she could capture the breadth of her role, Bancroft began visiting schools for deaf children, and soon learned of Dr.

Edna S. Levine, a well-known psychologist who worked with deaf clients. A meeting was set up between the two. Bancroft's intensity struck Levine, who encouraged her to study more about sign language, deafness, and the deaf community. A friendship ensued. And the meeting of these two women eventually changed the face of deaf theater in America.

Taras B. Denis, a deaf writer from New York, has said that these two women were the impetus behind the formation of the National Theatre of the Deaf. According to Denis,

> Miss Bancroft and Dr. Levine became fast friends, the outcome of which was something never before attempted. On the one hand, the unassuming academic mind of Dr. Levine: dedicated to the deaf, adept at the business of getting the public interested in their cultural needs, a personality with a penchant for convincing. On the other hand, the box office appeal of Miss Bancroft: dedicated to the theater, adept at the business of getting a different kind of interest from her public, a personality who came away from her own lessons in the language of signs convinced that the deaf have more to offer dramawise. And so, it was in the joining of these two separate forces that the traveling repertory theater had its genesis.[3]

Thus began the long, arduous battle for what would eventually become the National Theatre of the Deaf, better known by its abbreviation, NTD.

Levine had spent her professional life working in the field of deafness. At the time, she was a consulting psychologist at the Lexington School for the Deaf in New York City and a professor at New York University's Deafness Research and Training Center. Dr. Levine also had written numerous books on deafness and psychology, including *The Psychology of Deafness* (1960).

An avid playgoer, Levine often attended school plays performed by deaf children, as well as professional plays on Broadway. Her two passions, theater and the deaf community, led her to the notion of a professional theater troupe of deaf actors. And when Bancroft came her way, she seized the opportunity to put the wheels in motion.

When Bancroft sought reliable expertise in the field of deafness and sign language, Levine suggested that she visit deaf school programs and meet deaf adults. Because Levine was not considered a fluent signer herself,[4] she asked Martin L. A. Sternberg to teach Bancroft the language of signs. According to Sternberg, he tutored Bancroft for six months in New York City.[5] Bancroft, he later recalled, embraced her signing lessons "with intensity and great enthusiasm."[6]

Her enthusiasm was apparently infectious, and before long, two influential Broadway directors, Gene Lasko and Arthur Penn, and a set designer, David Hays, had been affected by her fervor. Gene Lasko, the director of the 1957 television version of *The Miracle Worker,* not only lent moral support but also later directed NTD productions. Arthur Penn, who directed Bancroft in the Broadway version of *The Miracle Worker,* as well as *Two for the Seesaw,* provided similar assistance until he returned to Hollywood in 1961.

Then there was David Hays, a prolific and highly successful Broadway set designer. He was best known as the leading designer for the Eugene O'Neill revivals of the fifties, including the American premiere of O'Neill's 1957 Pulitzer Prize–winning play *Long Day's Journey into Night.* Even before Bancroft persuaded him to get involved, Hays had been experimenting with a return to physical forms of expression in an attempt to revitalize the stage. He knew that the human body in itself was a source of drama, and he was unafraid of unconventional stage techniques.

Hays had no way of knowing how profoundly Bancroft's little project would affect his life and his career—he was destined to become NTD's founding artistic director, a post he has held since the theater's beginning. He remembers the excitement of more than thirty-four years ago:

Levine conceived the notion of the theatre of the deaf. She and Bancroft thought of *The Miracle Worker* as part of the scheme to get people, especially the federal government, interested. They got excited and they got me excited about it as a designer.[7]

David Hays was born in New York City in 1930. Eighteen years later, he graduated from Woodmere Academy in New York and entered Harvard College; he graduated magna cum laude in 1952 with an A. B. in the history of fine arts. During his undergraduate years at Harvard, Hays worked as a set designer for the Brattle Theater Company on such plays as Sheridan's *The Critic* and Molnar's *Liliom.* Upon graduation, Hays won a Fulbright Scholarship to the Old Vic in London. During his London sojourn in 1952, he worked with John Gielgud and Peter Brook on Otway's *Venice Preserved.* That fall, he entered Yale, spending a year there before transferring to Boston University, where he earned his M.F.A. in theatrical design.

After spending another year at the Yale School of Drama, Hays took various technical and designing jobs, leading him eventually to work with José Quintero on plays by Eugene O'Neill, among them *Long Day's Journey into Night,* which won a Pulitzer Prize in 1957. Four years later, Hays was involved with another Pulitzer Prize–winning play, *All the Way Home* by Tad Mosel.[8] (This play was later produced by NTD in the 1984–85 season.) His set and lighting designs were nominated for Tony Awards four times between 1960 and 1966.[9] He won Obie awards for Behan's *The Quare Fellow* (1958) and Genet's *The Balcony* (1959) and Rodgers's *No Strings* (1962). In 1977, Hays finally won his Tony, when NTD was recognized for theatrical excellence.

During the pre-NTD years, Hays designed sets and lights for the New York City Ballet, Boston Opera, Vivian Beaumont Theatre at Lincoln Center, and the Metropolitan Opera Association. Designing "ideal" theaters was another of his interests, taking him to Oklahoma City, where he codesigned the New Mummers Theatre for Mack Scism, who would later become NTD's tour manager.[10]

Hays's involvement with Japan started in 1960 when he was chosen as a technical consultant for the first Grand Kabuki tour of America. Ten years later, Hays designed the first American musical in Japan. In all, he has designed approximately 140 ballets, operas, and plays.[11] During this time, he met and married actress Leonora Landau and became the father of two children: Daniel in 1960 and Julie in 1964.

Hays's background in visual design never prepared him for directing a theater of the deaf. With the exception of a deaf linotypists' gathering at Harvard Square in the fifties, an experience that he thought of as an "oddity,"[12] Hayes had never encountered deaf people or sign language.

Although *The Miracle Worker* was not the first play with a deaf character, it was the first that used sign language as an expressive medium. One could argue, however, that the Gallaudet College Dramatic Club earned this distinction with its 1942 Broadway production of Joseph Kesselring's *Arsenic and Old Lace.* Under the leadership of Eric Malzkuhn, Gallaudet's production garnered good reviews. One insightful theater historian, Burns Mantle, proclaimed the performance to be a "harbinger of things to come."[13] But despite its unique performance, there was no immediate impact on American theater, nor on deaf theater, which would wait two more decades for attention to be focused on this art form.[14]

A number of twentieth-century plays had focused on the deafness or muteness of a central character. *Warnings* (1913) by Eugene O'Neill was the first modern American drama dealing with a main character, James Knapp, who becomes deaf.[15] The first modern play with a born-deaf central character was *Johnny Belinda* (1940). Eugene Ionesco's *The Chairs* (1952) is probably the best-known play to make use of a deaf character, who is chosen to serve symbolically as a spokesperson on the meaning of human existence.[16] *The Miracle Worker,* nonetheless, has been generally acknowledged as the breakthrough play in which sign language was given serious credence.

Gibson's play, a retelling of the early life of Helen Keller, was demanding—doubly so, because Bancroft had to learn to sign and fingerspell fluently to have the credibility necessary to carry the drama realistically on stage. And through this powerful, compelling story of human communication and the rich experiences she had while researching her role, Bancroft developed an empathy for deaf people.

She became so involved that she later received awards and recognition for her work on behalf of people with disabilities. And in 1961, she served as spokesperson for the thirty-third annual educational campaign of the American Hearing Society.

Bancroft's performance captured her audiences, and the play was a tremendous success. With a run of 700 performances,[17] it far surpassed previous plays involving a deaf character. Plans for the movie version were quickly put into motion.

Meanwhile, Levine had been patiently awaiting an opportunity to advance the notion of the deaf theater. She persisted. Setting the stage for her coup de theatre, Levine arranged for Bancroft and Penn to see the 1959 spring production of *Othello* at Gallaudet University, presented as part of the students' extracurricular activities.

Howard Palmer had the lead role in the Gallaudet production. So effective was his performance that the play was filmed for an NBC affiliate in Washington, D.C. This film became the first widely distributed documentary about Gallaudet's theatrical productions.

The emotive power of the language of signs was not lost on Bancroft and Penn as they watched Palmer and the cast of *Othello.* Both Broadway visitors were so taken with the beauty of the performance that they joined Levine in seeking a grant from the Vocational Rehabilitation Administration (VRA), which was headed at that time by another friend of the deaf community, Mary Switzer, in the Department of Health, Education, and Welfare. Switzer, long an advocate for deaf rights, must have been delighted when she was approached by Levine, Bancroft, and Penn. Her recollection of the first meeting was that

> Anne became very enamored of the possibility of using the theatre and signing simultaneously with speaking actors as a new form. She thought of this because the very year that she became absorbed in the problems of the deaf, she saw *Othello* done at Gallaudet and also Kabuki dancers from Japan, and these two things inspired her and Arthur Penn. Arthur Penn saw this as a way to crack the federal government's interest in putting money into the arts.[18]

Switzer's involvement with the deaf community went far beyond her job with the Department of Health, Education, and Welfare, where the programs she supervised had a major impact on the deaf community. In her capacity, she worked alongside Boyce R. Williams, the first deaf professional to work for the Rehabilitation Services Administration. Years after her initial meetings with Bancroft, she headed the Committee on the Role and Function of Gallaudet College as an Institution of Higher Learning for the Deaf. Under her leadership, this committee set the pace for formidable changes that would broaden the school's scope for years to come. Switzer also was instrumental in the development of the National Technical Institute for the Deaf (NTID) in Rochester, New York. Switzer's dedication to the deaf community earned her more than sixteen honorary degrees, including the following citation from the National Association of the Deaf (NAD): "[She has] given us the most precious gift that one can bestow upon man, the opportunity and the means to help ourselves."[19]

Despite the dedication of Switzer, Levine, Bancroft, and Penn, the grant application was not accepted. Funding did not become available for sign-language productions on Broadway, primarily because there was no organization that could be held accountable for the funds.[20] In fact, since Congress had abandoned the Federal Theater in 1939, no art project had received federal support.

Back in New York, Levine, Bancroft, and Penn pondered their next move. Lasko and Hays, too, were dismayed to learn the news. But each then became involved in his or her own work for the remainder of 1959 and all of 1960, and the project languished until 1961.

Meanwhile, Professor William C. Stokoe, Jr., head of the Gallaudet University English Department, wrote a precedent-setting book, *Sign Language Structure* (1960). The first to recognize American Sign Language (ASL) as a language in its own right, Stokoe's monograph marked a breakthrough.

Although sign language, or "manualism," has been in use for hundreds of years, originating in France and Spain, it has been viewed by many American hearing educators as "primitive" or "grotesque." Indeed, for more than a hundred years, a "methods war" has been bitterly raging in the United States over the use of sign language versus oral communication. The often bitter debates were intensified in the late nineteenth century by telephone inventor Alexander Graham Bell, who disapproved of sign language as an educational method for teaching deaf children. Bell espoused speech, speechreading, and auditory training as the most practical method for preparing deaf children for an oral/aural English-speaking society. His controversial stance caused an educational schism that has lasted more than one hundred years between the oral supporters and manual advocates.

The latter, comprised mostly of deaf people, felt culturally and socially threatened by the oral method. Consequently, the National Association of the Deaf was founded in 1880 to combat oralism and to protect the civil rights of deaf people. The Alexander Graham Bell Association for the Deaf, Inc., was largely viewed by the deaf community as an adversary fraught with paternalism and authoritarianism, while oralists, mostly hearing educators and parents, perceived the deaf community as being anti-English and antispeech.

Historically, it was not until the late 1960s and early 1970s that sign language started gaining acceptance as a primary means of giving deaf children an overall education. There was then a movement to Total Communication, which eventually led to a bilingual and bicultural movement in some residential and mainstream programs in the nineties.

Stokoe's work allowed ASL to "come out of the closet." The language of signs finally gained acceptance in academic and public circles and stimulated a surge in sign language books.

Then in 1960, Dr. Leonard Siger, a member of the Gallaudet University English department, wrote an article published in the *Johns Hopkins Magazine* about the potentiality of sign language on the stage. He wrote:

> Of course, the sign language of casual conversation is not appropriate to the stage. But sign language properly learned and properly used can be a vehicle of considerable power and beauty, better suited to the expression of emotion, in some respects, than any spoken language.[21]

Several other developments called attention to deaf people's needs and rights. The Fort Monroe [Virginia] Conference of 1961 sowed the seeds that sprouted many successful grants and enhanced the career goals of deaf people. This pivotal conference was aimed at getting more services for the deaf population. One result was a sense of unity among deaf and hearing people to provide more educational and social services, which had previously been unavailable. The Registry of Interpreters for the Deaf was formed a few years later to enable deaf and hearing people to interact in a variety of situations. And it was during that same period (1964) that Dr. Robert Weitbrecht successfully synchronized a teletypewriter machine with a telephone, thus allowing deaf people access to the telephone for the first time.

During the early part of 1960, the idea of a repertory theater for the deaf was discussed by Douglas Burke (a Gallaudet graduate) and George Detmold, Lou Fant, and Robert Panara, all faculty members at Gallaudet University. Their concept was merely a serious discussion that never materialized. Nearly a year later, Martin L. A. Sternberg wrote a paper espousing a similar idea. However, all these people later became integrally involved in NTD during its most formative years.

Though two years had passed since the grant had been declined, Bancroft had not lost her desire to see the power of sign language brought to the stage. When she learned of an upcoming Gallaudet production of Thornton Wilder's *Our Town,* she headed to Washington, this time with Hays in tow.

While in the nation's capital, Bancroft once again teamed with Levine to present a proposal for a deaf repertory theater to Mary Switzer. The proposal stated the following statistics:

> Three-quarters of the deaf adult male working population and three-fifths of the deaf working women are employed in manual occupations . . . manual occupation was, and still is, a "traditional vocation pigeonhole for the deaf." To break with this undesirable situation . . . something like a repertory theatre is needed.[22]

Hays later recalled the proposal and the visit to Washington:

> She (Levine) conceived it (NTD) as a social tool . . . seeing it as supplying role models, breaking up job pigeonholing . . . getting more opportunities to deaf people. It didn't work. . . . they didn't get additional funds from the government. Perhaps they concentrated too much on just one production.[23]

The second proposal missed another chance because of "lack of financial backing."[24] No one or group had guaranteed to match the federal government's grant.

But the trip was not in vain. Bancroft and Hays were impressed with *Our Town* under Dr. George Detmold's direction, and Hays realized that what Bancroft had said was absolutely true—that this was indeed a theatrical form to be explored. He says:

> I was very moved by George's production of that play. I felt it was very clean. I thought the actors in particular were very moving. There was something about sign language. The quiet communication. The sign and the voice together. The quiet way of speaking. I remember the speech about the stars. How poetically simple and beautifully acted that speech was. How it went. How the stars fade away and how we become like them . . . part of the universe again. It was very touching.[25]

A dedicated group of faculty members were the primary force behind the Gallaudet production. Dean George Detmold, Dr. Leonard Siger, and Professor Robert Panara assisted members of the Saturday Dramatics Club, an extracurricular club for students and faculty. Other members included Howard Palmer, Douglas Burke, and Gilbert Eastman, who became head of the Drama Department at Gallaudet in 1963.

Wilder's play was a perfect showcase for the Gallaudet group, with its simple language easily adaptable for sign language. The bare stage provided an ideal backdrop to demonstrate the superior signing and mime skills of the cast.

A mutual respect between Hays and Detmold was born. Hays recognized the professionalism in Detmold's work—his instincts for space and timing with sign language. They began a correspondence that would span many years, and in the course of this friendship, they developed a concept, a theory of how a sign-language theater might work.

However, despite the outstanding performance, after the second grant proposal failed, the New York group began to break up. Bancroft and Penn began preparing for the movie version of *The Miracle Worker* (1962). Penn had insisted on using Bancroft for the movie version, knowing how powerful her performances had been on stage. She would play to Patty Duke's Helen Keller.

Bancroft went on to give one of the most complex, powerful, and moving performances ever seen on film. She won the Academy Award for best actress, and the movie itself garnered four nominations, including best director, best screenplay, and best supporting actress, which Patty Duke won.

Lasko and Hays, too, went on to their respective directing and stage-designing projects in New York City.

The turning point for NTD came in 1962 when, by chance, theater executive George C. White became interested in a picturesque piece of property situated near the Long Island Sound, a favored sailing area of his. Located about five miles from New London, Connecticut, where Eugene O'Neill, one of America's foremost playwrights, had spent many childhood summers, the property included a mansion, a barn, and ninety-five acres of land. By 1963, White knew he wanted the property, but he was not exactly sure what he would do with it. The townspeople, however, had already conceived that this would be an ideal location for a theater center.

White called in a fellow theater professional and sailor, none other than David Hays. Hays realized that this could be the perfect home for the National Theatre of the Deaf. And White liked the idea.

Once again drawn into the possibility of getting the sign-language theater off the ground, Hays eagerly contacted Bancroft and Penn with the good news, only to find that their interest had waned. With busy Hollywood careers now in full sail, they chose not to get involved this time.

Despite the loss of Bancroft and Penn, Hays remained undeterred. He contacted Levine. She was still interested, and in no time she had set up a meeting with Mary Switzer. It was to be the first meeting between Hays and Switzer, and proved to be a productive one.

By this time, permission had been granted by Mrs. Carlotta O'Neill to use her husband's name: The Eugene O'Neill Center was waiting to become the home for NTD. Also home to other theater groups, the Eugene O'Neill Center, with thirteen different programs, has grown into a haven for budding playwrights, theater educators, actors, musicians, and other theatrical personnel.

Everything that was necessary to receive the grant for a sign-language theater was now in place. Levine wrote the planning grant in 1966.[26]

The third time was the charm, and $16,500 was set aside by the Rehabilitation Services Administration of the Department of Health, Education, and Welfare to cover the period from June 1, 1966, to March 1, 1967.[27]

The National Theatre of the Deaf would never have evolved without Switzer and her Vocational Rehabilitation Administration (VRA) colleagues, such as Boyce R. Williams, the highest-ranking deaf person in the federal government at the time; Edward C. Carney, deaf; Jim Moss, hearing; Edwin Martin, hearing; and Malcolm J. Norwood, also deaf. This team of deaf and hearing professionals combined insights and talents to sponsor many successful programs for deaf people during the sixties. The National Theatre of the Deaf is considered by this group to have been their most important project.[28] While support from NAD, Gallaudet, and the O'Neill Foundation had certainly helped to advance this lofty goal, it was the grants authorized by VRA that allowed the birth of NTD.

The money was allocated to finance an experimental production for Gallaudet. With Hays as managing director, Euripides' *Iphigenia in Aulis* was selected as the showcase to introduce the talented deaf actors, all of whom came from Gallaudet, to non-deaf theater professionals. The goal of the production was to prove that an all-deaf cast was capable of developing into a professional acting company that would appeal to a nonsigning hearing audience. The play was scheduled during the O'Neill

Center's second National Playwrights' Conference in the summer of 1966.

It was only natural that Hays would call in his confidante and collaborator, George Detmold. Detmold understood the power of the deaf actors and once said:

> [The deaf actor] may or may not need the kind of sensitivity training that is given to American actors these days. He usually learns fast, possibly because he is accustomed to express himself kinesthetically rather than vocally; and surprisingly, no matter how seriously he may suffer from stage fright, he is always perfectly composed on stage—again, possibly because of his language, he has a physical sense for his tensions.[29]

To this, Detmold added his personal theory about a deaf cast.

> A theater of deaf actors, in the medium of communication used by the deaf, has contributed to the American theater, and should have a brilliant future. There is poetics to the sign language also, and we must find signs with smooth and easy transitions. The question of poetics becomes extremely complicated when he comes to the chorus in a Greek tragedy. As you know, the choral odes in a Greek play were usually delivered to the accompaniment of music, the actors dancing as they spoke their lines. In our performances, the actors actually dance the sign language. The effect, we think, is well worth the trouble it takes to achieve, and makes a legitimate distinction between ordinary episodes of the play and the highly colored poetry of the choral odes.[30]

And so the stage was set for the first demonstration of the National Theatre of the Deaf. It remained to be seen how this new art form on the stage would be perceived by seasoned theater lovers. The deaf acting troupe faced a severe test before an audience of professional directors, actors, and critics in that summer of 1966.

But George White was optimistic. He predicted that the acting troupe would make "a new meaningful contribution by the deaf to the American performing arts."[31]

The Gallaudet actors were ready. Their drama club had been in existence since 1892, and a wealth of talent had graced those silent stages. With the exception of *Arsenic and Old Lace* in 1942 and *The Miser,*[32] a production that had traveled to Akron, Ohio, in 1949, Gallaudet performers had never demonstrated their skills before professionals, such as those gathering at the Eugene O'Neill Center.

The production was a hit. It was "met with enthusiasm for its beauty and uniqueness"[33] and a "a highly favorable response."[34] Deaf writer Taras B. Denis pronounced it a successful debut before professionals in every area of theater.[35]

With a sigh of relief and joy, Hays was then able to apply for another grant—this time for a three-year pilot project designed to set up a touring company of deaf performers. A stream of advisers, hearing and deaf, came to Waterford to assist with the planning.

The National Association of the Deaf (NAD) threw its full support behind the concept of NTD. During their twenty-eighth biennial convention in San Francisco in 1966, they passed a resolution encouraging cooperation between the O'Neill Center and the NAD.[36] Dr. Robert Sanderson of Utah, president of NAD from 1964 to 1968, believed in connecting with the nonsigning hearing world as a matter of public relations. Sanderson not only supported the grant application made to the VRA, but recruited two more people to help Hays: Douglas Burke and Jesse M. Smith.

Burke, the director of NAD's Cultural Program, had written and directed a few plays himself. Although he had not found a producer for his material, in 1961 he produced one of his own plays, *The Good Peddler,* for the District of Columbia Club for the Deaf. Jesse M. Smith of Indiana, the editor of the NAD publication, the *Deaf American,* was also enlisted by NAD to assist Hays.

Taras B. Denis, whose highly popular "Front Row Center" column appeared regularly in the *Deaf American,* provided a steady flow of news about NTD.

The cover of the *Deaf American*'s January 1967 issue boasted a full-size photograph of David Hays. Showing Hays with his hands on a large blueprint, the story, "The Origin and Concept of the Proposed National Repertory Theatre for the Deaf," was written by Bert Shaposka. Covering the trials and tribulations of the NTD and how it had all started, Shaposka also credited Douglas Burke and Bernard Bragg for their roles as consultants to the O'Neill Foundation.[37]

With the growing momentum, it became abundantly clear that the general public should be exposed to this type of theater. George White contacted NBC television officials. An agreement was struck to tape a pilot project in the barn at the O'Neill Center.[38] The one-hour show for NBC's "Experiment in Television" was taped in February 1967. Nanette Fabray, a popular actress who had a hearing loss, hosted the NBC special, which was written by Gene Lasko and directed by Richard Schneider.

Upon advice from members of the deaf community, Hays invited a group of experienced deaf performers to participate in the project. Included in this early group of consultants, mostly products of Gallaudet, were Dr. Robert Panara, Eric Malzkuhn, Taras B. Denis, Douglas Burke, Bernard Bragg, Gilbert Eastman, and Lou Fant, the hearing son of deaf parents.

Among those selected to perform were Bernard Bragg, Gilbert Eastman, June (Russi) Eastman, Audree Norton, Ralph White, Phyllis Frelich, and Howard Palmer.[39] Bragg had recruited or recommended most of these people to serve as actors and consultants. Hays not only approved the choices but also had a hand in convincing Fant, Panara, and others to participate in the television experiment. Fant was chosen as the hearing "reader" for the deaf performers. His job was to translate the deaf actors' lines for the nonsigning hearing audience.

Well after the rehearsals were under way, shock waves emanated throughout the deaf community, the NBC offices, and Congress.

When the newspapers announced NBC's special program on NTD, the first major production using sign language on television,[40] an objection arose from the Alexander Graham Bell (AGB) Association, Inc., two weeks before the show was to air.

This was the first time Hays had experienced the schism between the signing and the oral deaf, and he was stunned by this shocking turn of events. So earnest was his involvement in the development of the theater that he had been unaware of the age-old clash of educational methods. He phoned Levine to ask what was going on, to which she replied, "Oh, David, I didn't want to tell you about this dispute—I thought it might discourage you."[41] Hays and NBC were astonished by the text of the telegram, which read,

> To NBC: . . . we are opposed to any programming which indicates that the use of the language of signs is inevitable for deaf children or it is anything more than an artificial language, and a foreign one at that, for the deaf of this country.[42]

Copies of the telegram were sent to almost everyone in Congress. Worded as it was, it was as if this telegram reflected the sentiments of all decent people throughout America.

Aghast at this unexpected reaction, NBC officials turned to Hays for help. With the backing of the deaf community, Hays responded to the AGB that "such television programs bring enormous cultural benefit to the deaf who are deprived of theatre." He added that the programs would show "highly gifted deaf people working in a developed art form of great beauty."[43]

NBC went ahead with the program with four members of the Broadway group who had pushed for the concept of the theater of the deaf directing the special—Gene Lasko, Arthur Penn, Richard Schneider, and Joe Layton. The 1967 telecast included scenes from *Hamlet, All the Way Home,* and three Broadway musicals—*Guys and Dolls, Kismet,* and *South Pacific.*

During the taping, the O'Neill Center received news from Switzer and the VRA that a three-year grant of $331,000 had been awarded to the foundation.[44] As the new managing director of the newest acting company in America, Hays wasted no time. He began making plans to set up a drama school for promising actors and company personnel, employ a staff of theater professionals to assist in their training, and begin conducting rehearsals for a professional touring company.[45]

After the O'Neill Center took a percentage of the grant, NTD received $105,000 from VRA and $40,000 from the Office of Education, under Jim Moss.[46]

It had taken eight years of perseverance, from 1959 to 1967, to achieve a breakthrough for NTD, culminating with a successful TV debut and a major grant. No single factor was responsible for NTD's inception. However, the importance of the early interest from Bancroft, Levine, and other Broadway people cannot be underestimated. Four plays from Gallaudet University had also left a lasting impression on the people who eventually endorsed a professional theater of the deaf. The deaf community, including the NAD, supported NTD. Then there was David Hays, who depended upon both deaf and hearing individuals, as well as groups such as the O'Neill Center, to form NTD. Hays had a vision, but he was not alone.

An untested but talented group of deaf actors would bear the responsibility of proving that sign language deserved a place on the American stage.

Hays began developing NTD into a traveling company. From the beginning, he had realized that the theater needed the national exposure that only a traveling company could command, and had planned from the start to make this a touring company, rather than a repertory theater.

In 1967 thirty-five deaf people from all over the country were invited to the O'Neill Center.[47] This inaugural group included the original television crew and some new members: Violet Armstrong, Charles Corey, Mary Beth Miller, Timothy Scanlon, Andrew Vasnick, Joe Velez, Joyce Flynn Lasko (Broadway actress and wife of Gene Lasko), and Will Rhys, an acting student. Ed Fearon became the musician, playing the innovative Baschet instruments, which are vibrating sheet metals. The vibrating sheet metals cue most of the actors as well as set the tension or mood of the play.

In order to prepare this group for the stage, Hays invited Broadway directors to train and to rehearse the company for its first tour. Hays reminded himself of what his theater colleague Tyrone Guthrie had told him, "Don't get involved in pantomime or any of those forms. Use the language and ornate it. Language is our glory." With such advice in mind, Hays wanted the deaf actors to prove that sign language could add a new dimension to the stage.[48]

Just before embarking on the maiden tour, Hays told the company,

> You understand, our object is not to create just another theatre for the deaf. Our new theatre is for everybody. It is a mistake to assume that deaf talent has no place in the world of entertainment. It does—and we're going to prove it.[49]

Taras B. Denis eloquently captured the essence of the journey ahead:

> All told, the new theatre—the showboat of the nation's deaf—has been launched. Commissioned, but yet unchristened, she floats in port: Proud, the promise of potential in her planks, confident that her captain will come up with a crew capable of challenging the often rough seas of the entertainment world. How will she sail? What storms will she weather? What ports will she visit? What cargo will she unload? Above all, what new dramatic adventures will she be able to add in the log of her sister ships already on these seas? Not just time, but tide, too, will tell.[50]

NOTES

1. Dorothy Miles, "A History of Theatre Activities in the Deaf Community of the United States," Master's thesis, Connecticut College, 1974, 51.

2. Miles, 24.

3. Taras B. Denis, "Repertory Theatre for Deaf Launched with NYU-Sponsored Playwriting Contest," *The Deaf American* (December 1966): 26.

4. Robert Panara, interview with author, April 24, 1988.

5. Martin Sternberg, interview with author, June 24, 1988.

6. Sternberg interview.

7. David Hays, interview with author, March 10, 1988.

8. Mike Kaplan, ed., *Variety Presents: The Complete Book of Major U.S. Show Business Awards* (New York: Garland Publishing, 1985), 409.

9. Hays interview.

10. NTD Tour Brochure, 1987–88, 35.

11. Hays interview.

12. Hays interview.

13. Stephen C. Baldwin, "Broadway 1942: *Arsenic and Old Lace,* A Signed Production Ahead of Its Time," *The Voice* (November/December 1989): 20–22.

14. Miles, 10.

15. John V. Van Cleve, ed., *Gallaudet Encyclopedia of Deaf People and Deafness,* s.v. "Dramatic Characters in Literature," by Catherine Elmes-Kalbacher (New York: McGraw-Hill, 1987), 162.

16. Ibid.

17. Henry Hewes, ed., *The Best Plays of 1962–1963* (New York: Dodd, Mead, and Company, 1963), 367.

18. George McClendon, "The Unique Contribution of the National Theatre of the Deaf to the American Theatre," Master's thesis, Catholic University, 1972, 8.

19. Jack Gannon, *Deaf Heritage: A Narrative History of Deaf America* (Silver Spring, Md.: National Association of the Deaf, 1981), 338.

20. McClendon, 9.

21. Leonard Siger, "The Silent Stage," *The Johns Hopkins Magazine* (October 1960): 12.

22. Denis, 26.

23. Hays interview.

24. Denis, 26.

25. Hays interview.

26. Dorothea Dodd, interview with author, April 9, 1988.

27. McClendon, 11.

28. Robert Panara and John Panara, *Great Deaf Americans* (Silver Spring, Md.: T. J. Publishers, 1982), 70.

29. George Detmold, untitled and unpublished paper (presentation made in 1967) (Washington, D.C.: Gallaudet University Archives), 9.

30. Detmold, 7.

31. Miles, 11.

32. Nancy B. Tadie, "A History of Drama at Gallaudet College: 1864 to 1969," Ph.D. diss., New York University, 1978, 219.

33. John M. Heidger, "The Theatre of the Deaf in America: The Silent Stage," Master's thesis, 1979, Southern Illinois University, 44.

34. Miles, 56.

35. Denis, 26.

36. Bert Shaposka, "The Origin and Concept of the Proposed National Repertory Theatre for [sic] the Deaf," *The Deaf American* (February 1967): 7.

37. Shaposka, 7.

38. McClendon, 58.

39. McClendon, 59.

40. Gannon, 346.

41. Hays, personal tape, June 20, 1992.

42. Gannon, 346.

43. Gannon, 346.

44. Lewis Funke, "Theatre of Deaf Gets U.S. Funds: Grant Will Enable Troupe To Be Established," *New York Times,* February 25, 1967, 13.

45. Denis, 27.

46. Hays interview, June 1992.

47. McClendon, 60–61.

48. Hays interview, June 1992.

49. Hays interview, March 1988.

50. Denis, 6.

The National Theatre of the Deaf Presents

THE DYBBUK

Between Two Worlds

CHAPTER 2

Behind the Scenes

*M*ajor tasks faced Hays and his small band of consultants, which included some of the most talented theatrical people in the deaf community: Bernard Bragg, Robert Panara, Eric Malzkuhn, and Douglas Burke. With the first tour slated for the fall of 1967, there was little time to prepare. They began by recruiting company members and translators.

Hays knew that finding the right combination of actors to launch the troupe was one of the most important tasks ahead of him. Not only did he need to find actors but also reliable and experienced translators.

Deaf text translators played a key role during the first three years of experimentation. English-language texts were subjected to rigorous translation, and the translators had to know the right signs to match the English words, both in context and spirit.

Douglas Burke, Eric Malzkuhn, and Robert Panara began translating poems and plays into signs for the NTD and also served as sign masters for the casts. Eventually, company members like Patrick Graybill, Dorothy Miles, Bernard Bragg, and Andrew Vasnick would also become involved with the translation of NTD works.

Bernard Bragg played a vital role during the experimental years. He was the only deaf performer with professional experience. He had trained as a mime with Marcel Marceau and he had his own television show, "The Quiet Man," in San Francisco, from 1958 to 1961. Bragg also recruited many of the original NTD company members for David Hays.

As expected, Gallaudet proved to be a rich source of talent for the fledgling company. Nearly all of the company's deaf performers had originally attended college there. Hearing actors were selected more for their vocal range and ability to learn signs than for their acting, though all of them had been trained professionally in acting.

Seventeen people made up the original troupe.

Violet Armstrong, a talented wardrobe person, was from New York and was a product of the grass-roots theaters. She, like Bernard Bragg, had performed for the New York Theatre Guild. At this writing, Armstrong is a resident in Dallas, Texas, where she is actively involved in deaf senior-citizen activities.

Charles Corey, who now resides in California, had been a newspaper worker.[1] Corey's daughter, Rita, later became a company member from 1977 to 1979.

Gilbert Eastman and his wife, June Russi, had maintained an interest in drama, first as actors at Gallaudet, and then Gilbert went on to become a drama instructor and cohost on the Emmy Award–winning show "Deaf Mosaic." After thirty-five illustrious years at Gallaudet, Gilbert retired in 1992.

Phyllis Frelich, who was studying at Gallaudet to become a librarian, had acted with the Eastmans. Joining the NTD forever changed the direction of Frelich's career. She won a Tony Award in 1980 for her portrayal of Sarah in *Children of a Lesser God,* and is now well known in Hollywood for her various roles in television productions, including "Love Is Never Silent." Frelich made history when she became the first deaf person to serve on the board of the Screen Actors Guild in Hollywood.

Mary Beth Miller, who later taught William Hurt how to sign as he prepared for his role in the movie version of *Children of a Lesser God,* was also studying library science. Miller has made her mark in the deaf community as a comedienne, traveling throughout the country to meet the demand for her deaf humor. Miller has also written several sign-language books.

Audree Norton had been teaching deaf children and adults for several years when she was tapped for a position with the NTD. She would be the first deaf member to land a role tailored for hearing audiences on television, with a part on "Mannix." Norton later became an activist of sorts, protesting the use of hearing actors to portray deaf people. Her dissension over the selection of Amy Irving for the role of a deaf woman in the movie *Voices* blacklisted her in Hollywood, and her career was cut short as a result. After teaching English and drama for a number of years at Ohlone College in Fremont, California, she retired in 1992.

Howard Palmer also taught deaf children prior to joining the NTD troupe. He was well known for his Shakespearean roles at Gallaudet, as well as for the drama program he established at the Mississippi School for the Deaf.

Tim Scanlon, a promising young actor, was hired while still a student at Gallaudet, where he was the football team mascot and a cross-country runner. He took a year off from Gallaudet to join NTD, later returning to school before going back to NTD, where he played the lead in many productions.

Andrew Vasnick had been the dean of students at New York School for the Deaf after teaching at Gallaudet University for many years. He continued with the NTD company as an actor and director of the NTD Professional Theatre School until 1991.

Joe Velez was a linotypist, as well as an artist and athlete. His abiding passion for the theater proved to be a vital part of this talented crew, earning rave reviews from critics for his signed rendition of "Jabberwocky" in the first tour. Velez's career was cut short when he was struck down with cancer in 1975.

Ralph White, unlike the other original cast members, who stayed for three or more years, stayed for only a few months. White is remembered by Hays as a "terrifically talented actor."[2] White later served as a drama coach in programs for deaf children. Multitalented, White has also been a teacher, counselor, and later, superintendent of the Oklahoma School for the Deaf. At this writing, he is in Texas where he is a consultant, school board member, advocate, and active senior citizen.

Lou Fant, a hearing company member, was the son of deaf parents. An extraordinary signer, he was working at the Kendall School, a model elementary program at Gallaudet, and had already written three books on ASL when he joined the NTD group. Fant has led a colorful career, including a number of television and movie appearances.

Will Rhys, also hearing, was just finishing his bachelor's degree at Wesleyan University in Connecticut, where he studied acting and theatrical production.

Ed Fearon, a budding musician, was also part of the original troupe for the fall touring season.

Joyce Flynn Lasko, an established actress and wife of director Gene Lasko, was the fourth hearing person to join the troupe.

During the experimental years, NTD was expanded to include seven more deaf performers—recent graduates of Gallaudet or professionals in fields related to deafness.

One of these, Linda Bove, is now internationally known as "Linda the Librarian" on the Public Broadcasting System's "Sesame Street." Edward Waterstreet, Bove's husband, also became a part of the troupe. An all-around athlete, Waterstreet eventually became a director for NTD and elsewhere, as well as performing a leading role in the Emmy Award–winning television movie "Love Is Never Silent" (1985). At this writing, he is artistic director of Deaf West Theatre Company, established in 1991 and comprising a band of talented deaf actors and actresses in Los Angeles.

Richard Kendall, a Canadian, had majored in library science at Gallaudet. After leaving NTD, he assisted with the Tony Award–winning play *Children of a Lesser God* (1980) on Broadway as a stage manager and understudy, and later was a consultant and actor for the film version (1984).

Freda Norman joined directly after graduating from Gallaudet. Norman was destined to become a star in a San Francisco television program for deaf and hearing children, "Rainbow's End." Known largely for her role in "Supersign Woman," a deaf version of "Wonder Woman," she has remained active in theater circles since leaving NTD. At this writing, she, too, is with the Deaf West Theatre Company in Los Angeles.

Morton Steinberg, a deaf actor from California, stayed with the company for à short time as a wardrobe person.

Peter (Wechsberg) Wolf became America's first significant deaf filmmaker, producing *Deafula,* an innovative take-off on *Dracula,* and *Think Me Nothing.* Wolf was also a product of then Gallaudet.

Patrick Graybill, a brilliant leading actor and teacher, became an administrator for NTD and subsequently joined the drama department at NTID (National Technical Institute for the Deaf) in Rochester, New York. Graybill has remained active on the theater circuit, traveling the country in a one-man show. While working with Deaf West Theatre Company in 1991, he teamed up with Phyllis Frelich for their second staging of *The Gin Game.* (Their first staging took place in 1979.)

Dorothy Miles, who was born in Wales but spent most of her life in England, was a multitalented "Jill" of all trades—actress, director, playwright, historian, designer, and critic of deaf American theater.

Four hearing readers/actors joined NTD before 1970. They were John Basinger, Carol Fleming, Jacqueline Awad, and Corine Broskett. All had been trained in acting, directing, and music.

Selecting the original cast for the acting company was one of the most important tasks facing Hays. From the beginning and through the years, he has relied heavily on the input of company members before making final decisions. His method of selecting actors, though simple, is based on the long-range needs of the company. He comments on his method:

> [We need] someone who will look bigger on stage, who will be able to take attention . . . those who are bigger and larger than life. I've had very few run-ins with actors, more with hearing than deaf actors, and I've encouraged them (hearing) to leave the company. It's just a gut feeling. But it is also instinct and difficult and impossible to describe who will become a fine actor. I've been pretty lucky over the years.[3]

Since the selection of the first seventeen cast members, more than one hundred actors have joined the company. Many have remained longer than five years, and most have grown as performers; many have remained with the company.

As the new troupe evolved, new techniques were tried. When performing a text of great plays and poems, sign-mime was used, giving sign language, particularly American Sign Language, newly invented theatrical signs that were used to project the given text. Both the ASL and theatrical mime signs were "extended and dramatized into an art form that carried tremendous visual impact for those who simultaneously heard the words."[4] Many of the theatrical signs were given special shadings or movements, depending on the type of play and the particular moment.

Hays brought a new art form to life onstage—keeping all actors, including readers, onstage, rather than placing the speaking actors offstage, as had always been done at Gallaudet. Prior to NTD, voice actors had been called "readers," and they vocalized the script from offstage, using a microphone. They read from the script as they watched the play.

Voice actors reverse-interpret for each character, as well as play their own roles. They must think of language in different ways—and how to manifest it with the body and eyes. Voice actors must also become aware of using other senses, either simultaneously or singly; consequently, performers must develop great concentration.

Unfortunately, there are no understudies for voice actors, and one of their occupational hazards is that their voices can weaken, just as a deaf actor may have to cope with a sore hand or arm. In plays that sometimes have the atmosphere of a three-ring circus, such as NTD's *Volpone* (1978), voice actors must work with great vocal skill and energy. And while they are on the stage throughout the entire play, they must remain as inconspicuous as possible. If a deaf actor must sign alone onstage, the voice actor moves behind a prop or screen to voice the lines. They are both there—yet not there.

The simultaneous use of both deaf and voice actors is an unusual aesthetic element, but once the hearing audience grows accustomed to the style, there is a oneness of voice and sign. For example, a nonsigning voice actor might be humming, speaking, or chanting. For one poster, an artist's rendering, Linda Bove used a fingered rabbit sign, with a hearing rabbit, indicated by her left hand, listening to the voice actor, while her right hand represented a deaf rabbit that is watching the deaf signer, Joseph Sarpy, thus creating a unique oneness of voice and sign that the audience can *see* and *hear.*

Another integral component of NTD is movement. Besides being a visual language theatre, NTD's performers move a great deal. In addition to all the physical signing, the cast also develops ensemble movement and action. It is not unusual for the entire company to create a visual prop, such as a schooner, or to suggest a sign in order to enhance the atmosphere of the play. The actors might use the same sign for something such as "rain coming," yet each might accompany it with a different physical reaction. They might use the same facial expression to show a uniformly gleeful response to the rain. This overt physicalness has been heavily used in plays such as *Volpone*.

The pace of the signing during a performance is much faster than in normal signing, which is the essence of sign-language theater as opposed to deaf theater. The performers had wanted to develop a visual and physical language that would enrich the English text by simultaneously combining the theatricalized signs with onstage voices. Though aesthetically satisfying, this fast-paced signing often confused deaf playgoers accustomed to signing at a different pace and with a different style.

Early translators and original company members knew their innovative techniques would take time to perfect, and though it was initially frustrating for deaf playgoers, the deaf audiences eventually came to accept theatrical signs as something like a dialect or extension of ordinary signs.

Once his cast was lined up, Hays had one month to rehearse before NTD launched its first tour. He selected a variety of well-known short works to showcase the new art form and tapped two from the original Broadway group to direct.

Gene Lasko came in to direct William Saroyan's *The Man with His Heart in the Highlands*. John Hirsch directed *Tyger! Tyger! and Other Burnings,* a collection of poems. Japanese director Yoshio Aoyane directed Tsuruya Namboku's Kabuki play, *The Tale of Kasane*. And lastly, Joe Layton came back to direct a nonoperatic production of Puccini's *Gianni Schicchi*. Sculptured musical instruments designed by François and Bernard Baschet were used to accompany the four pieces. These instruments sometimes cued the deaf actors with vibrations and served as incidental music for the hearing audiences.

The first tour included performances in eighteen different cities along the Eastern Seaboard. Not all was smooth sailing, however; critics and audiences panned *The Man with His Heart in the Highlands. National Observer* reviewer Marion Simon called it too verbal, causing the play to take on "a jerky quality as the actors furiously move their hands in order to sign the words that the readers are saying."[5] Hays reacted quickly. Recognizing that the play was badly done, he strengthened the second tour by replacing Saroyan's play with Chekhov's comical monologue *On the Harmfulness of Tobacco.* Alvin Epstein was brought in to direct it.

On the original tour, *The Tale of Kasane* received favorable response. Critics felt that Japanese Kabuki plays were ideal for NTD. Critic Simon reported that the company "gracefully captures the classic simplicity of the Japanese Kabuki drama."[6]

Encouraged by the positive feedback, NTD incorporated Oriental theater into its future repertoire, gracing the stage with Japanese dancing in its summer programs. Later, Hays invited deaf Japanese actors to perform with NTD, and made successful tours in Japan and China.

Joe Velez, with Lou Fant voicing Lewis Carroll's collection of poems in *Jabberwocky,* and Audree Norton, coupled with Joyce Flynn Lasko to voice Browning's *How Do I Love Thee,* both earned favorable reviews as this new concept was brought to life. Elliott Norton of Boston's *Record American* wrote of their presentations,

> New in concept though not in text are poems which their narrators read in one brief interlude while the magnificent mimes of the company stand, move, gesture or stride to bring them vividly, tenderly, or hilariously to new life in a new and astonishing way.[7]

Taking his cues from his audiences and critics, Hays made poetry, especially that of Dylan Thomas, another popular part of the NTD repertory.

The final play of the program, a nonoperatic version of Puccini's *Gianni Schicchi* in which Bernard Bragg played the lead, was also highly successful. One observer wrote, "The copious movement of a full cast was sweeping and stylized with an underlying military precision that never had the right flank wondering what the left flank was doing."[8]

The overall reaction of the critics and reviews was enthusiastic.[9] *Time* offered a good example of the consensus:

> The dramatic program—ranging from Kabuki plays to slapstick to poetry reading—is broad enough to challenge the resources of any normal theatrical group. Yet none of the principal actors of the National Theatre of the Deaf utters a word, and only one actor can hear. No matter, the pacing and the performance are mistakable [*sic*] professional, and the critical notices are in the rave category.[10]

The troupe was on course, despite a few rough waters. According to Hays,

> The critics rate a large share of responsibility for our initial success. Our first performances at Wesleyan [University] and Williams [College] attracted crowds of forty—but so quickly did the words of Norton and Hirsch (*Boston Herald Traveler*) reach ahead, that even on our first tour we sold out eleven of our last twelve performances.[11]

Hays always sought to prevent the mass media, especially the theater critics, from viewing NTD with condescension because of the actors' deafness. He pointed out time and again to the press that the issue was the professionalism of the production and the artistic merit of NTD.

Indeed, hearing playgoers seemed unconcerned with the issue of deafness. John B. Welch, editor of *Baker's Plays* in Boston, summarized the reactions as follows:

> I see NTD as a whole art form. Like a picture on a wall. I do not think of the hearing actors as being hearing or the deaf actors as being deaf. I experience the performance as an art form per se because I am able to bring out the aesthetic soul in me. Thanks to the beauty of the art form in question. I am able to experience the impact of the whole aesthetic process.[12]

Helen Powers, a critic and early historian of NTD, wrote that

It didn't take long before the viewer no longer saw "signing" as such, but, rather graceful finger interpretations that enhanced the actions and the voices, hands that spoke and bodies whose rhythm accentuated the meaning. One lost all awareness of "deafness" and basked solely in the pleasures of a new and dynamic art form.[13]

The press dubbed NTD's style a new art form, commenting on the beauty of movement—an enhancement of art. *Time* magazine said, "They paint pictures in the air; it is language."[14]

Some critics, though, complained that NTD did not fulfill its potential because without the spoken words of the onstage voice actors, the nondeaf audience would understand little.

Some deaf playgoers, too, expressed unhappiness with NTD. Robert A. Halligan, in a letter published in the *Deaf American,* accused hearing people of exploiting the deaf and their sign language.[15] Elizabeth Lawder, a Gallaudet student, wrote an open letter in the student publication, *The Buff and Blue,* in 1969 and complained that NTD was not "deaf" enough for the deaf audience.[16] Halligan and Lawder expressed the sentiments of many in the grass-roots deaf community who felt that NTD was not an expression of their culture. Troupe member Dorothy Miles stated in her thesis, "A History of Theatre Activities in the Deaf Community" (1974), "For deaf persons, to whom signs were a means of communication, the impact of sign-mime, as it was called, was mainly one of incomprehension. Consequently, there was much dissatisfaction with, and in some cases resentment against the new theatre with the deaf community."[17]

Undeterred, Hays stayed the course with his selection of plays. He reminded detractors of the essence of NTD:

We have tried to choose works which stimulated both hearing and deaf audiences (not to be confused with "easy" for either group). When we chose one that was a particular challenge for deaf people, we tried to balance it with a less demanding play. Perhaps characteristically of all theatre audiences, the complaints were about the harder-to-follow one, with little recognition of the easier one.[18]

Reiterating the premise of NTD, Hays reminded the naysayers that "this is not, let me repeat, not a theatre for the deaf. It's a theatre of the deaf, just as the name says: a new form of theatre, aimed at general audiences, but always to remain intelligible to the deaf."[19]

The basic difference between theater *of* the deaf and theater *for* the deaf is the selection of script and the kind of audience. In theater *of* the deaf, which is also known as sign-language theatre, scripts about the hearing world as written by mostly hearing writers are selected. English is translated into sign language, sometimes stylized or theatricalized for expressive or artistic reason. Theater *for* the deaf, which is also called deaf theater, focuses on scripts about deaf people or deaf culture and utilizes deaf actors who use mostly American Sign Language.

Those first three years were indeed a time of learning, frustration, and growth for all who followed NTD. Though Hays had to counteract negative criticism on a regular basis, the media were generally favorable toward NTD's performances, and other negative criticism abated as the years passed.

Behind the scenes, NTD solved some of its public relations problems by assisting with the establishment of other theaters of the deaf, nourishing deaf playwrights, and developing original works based on the bona fide deaf perspective as part of the NTD repertoire. The general public liked what NTD was doing, and bookings continued to increase with each touring season.

Ralph White vividly recalls the inaugural tour in the fall of 1967.

How can I ever forget the experience! Although we practically lived out of a suitcase, the excitement made us forget the tedious traveling. We were not accustomed to being stage stars as real professionals. Our last stop for the fall tour was at Gallaudet. What a triumph, another standing ovation.[20]

The second tour included forty cities, as opposed to eighteen cities during the first tour. In its second season, 1968–69, the repertoire consisted of three pieces: Sheridan's *The Critic,* García Lorca's *The Love of Don Perlimplin and Belisa in the Garden,* and selected poems presented under the title *Blueprints.* It was during this season that NTD received its first award, The Outer Circle Drama Critics Award. Press reviews continued to be favorable as the young company weaved its way into American theater.

The third season became a turning point because of a major play that earned Broadway's respect. One of NTD's programs that year, a condensed version of Dylan Thomas's *Songs from Milk Wood,* directed by J Ranelli, received high praise from the theater world. According to Dorothy Miles, the *Milk Wood* production firmly established NTD in the critics' high estimation. Ironically, it was the least popular that year with deaf audiences.[21] The second production, Molière's *Sganarelle,* was also well received by most critics.

Though only three years old, by the 1969–70 season, NTD had given birth to another theater of the deaf: The Little Theatre of the Deaf (LTD) was given a place in the world with its own set of goals and bookings. The decision to establish LTD was based on the need to tour schools as well as to encourage drama programs for deaf students. Unlike its parent company, which was intended for adults, LTD sought to educate and entertain children with stories, poems, songs, and other group activities, all in sign language.

The National Theatre of the Deaf was surviving; the experiment had succeeded. Although there were some who felt that NTD had gotten off on the wrong foot by catering to a hearing audience and ignoring the deaf community, the goals were very much intact. The most important of these goals was to never be less than a first-rate professional acting company. Once again, deaf critic/philosopher Taras B. Denis captured NTD's position:

> In its search for a place in the sun of the entertainment world, the NTD is reflecting a good part of the rays into the everyday world of the deaf community. Thanks to its tours, television appearances and numerous other media of public exposure, more and more people from all walks of life—employers, especially average citizens no less—are coming to accept us for what we are: individuals, not a collective mystique.[22]

Mary Switzer, in evaluating NTD's critical first three years, saw that the social and vocational goals that had initially earned NTD's grant from the federal government were being accomplished. Her reaction was that

> There is a great lesson for all of us in the amazing approbation that the National Theatre of the Deaf has encountered everywhere. Glowing reviews in sophisticated theatrical publications, daily papers and periodicals underscore that manual language can introduce a new art form of great interest to the public.[23]

While NTD completed its initial tours, two events were taking place that would make NTD's work easier in the future. In 1968 two professional educators, Roy Holcomb and David Denton, introduced a new approach to deaf education called Total Communication, in which children would learn to use every possible communication form—signing, lipreading, speech, and mime. Sign language was beginning to be recognized as a legitimate tool for teaching deaf children.

The other event that benefited NTD was the growing popularity of sign language. Quality sign-language books were making their way into bookstores across the country. Books such as Lou Fant's *Say It With Hands,* Douglas O. Watson's *Talk With*

Your Hands, Lottie Riekehof's *Talk to the Deaf,* and Terrence J. O'Rourke's *A Basic Course in Manual Communication* were bought mainly by hearing Americans who wanted to learn how to communicate in the language of signs.

By 1970, NTD surely had the wind in its sails. Deaf actors and actresses dreamed of joining NTD. Hearing performers, too, sought recruitment by the small but prestigious company. And the Little Theatre of the Deaf had broken new ground.

The long journey, nevertheless, was only beginning. The young company understood what audiences expected. The reviews, critics, and publicity had helped shape the future productions of NTD. Yet, while the troupe had earned professional respect, the deaf community was still leery of an acting company with hearing people at the helm. And, they had not yet grown accustomed to the fast-paced theatrical signs.

As the country entered the seventies, NTD was faced with new artistic challenges. Requests to perform overseas began to come in, and there was a growing recognition that they would need to develop original works from within their own ranks.

NOTES

1. "NTD Founders: Where Are They Now?" *Deaf Life* trial issue (1987): 19.

2. David Hays, interview with author, March 10, 1988.

3. Hays interview.

4. Dorothy Miles, "A History of Theatre Activities in the Deaf Community of the United States," Master's thesis, Connecticut College, 1974, 61.

5. Marion Simon, "A Theater of the Deaf: Mime, Movement, and Signs Carry the Message," *National Observer,* October 9, 1967, 8.

6. Simon, 21.

7. Elliot Norton, "New Deaf Actors' Troupe Great in Premiere Show," *Record American,* September 25, 1967, 8.

8. Helen Powers, *Signs of Silence* (New York: Dodd, Mead, and Company, 1972), 128.

9. Powers, 126.

10. John Heidger, "The Theatre of the Deaf in America: The Silent Stage," Master's thesis, Southern Illinois University, 1979, 47–48.

11. Heidger, 49.

12. John Welch, interview with author, June 27, 1986.

13. Powers, 127.

14. "Pictures in the Air," *Time,* October 27, 1967, 4–5.

15. Robert A. Halligan, letter, *Deaf American* (February 1970): 41.

16. Elizabeth Lawder, "An Open Letter to the Theater of the Deaf," *The Buff and Blue,* April 24, 1969, 4.

17. Miles, 61.

18. Miles, 62.

19. Miles, 62.

20. Ralph White, interview with author, January 5, 1992.

21. Miles, 62.

22. Taras B. Denis, "Front Row Center: A Better Image? G'Wan Who Needs Them?" *Deaf American* (July/August 1967): 38.

23. Denis, 38.

The National Theatre of the Deaf *performs* Robert Louis Stevenson's

T R E A S U R E   I S L A N D

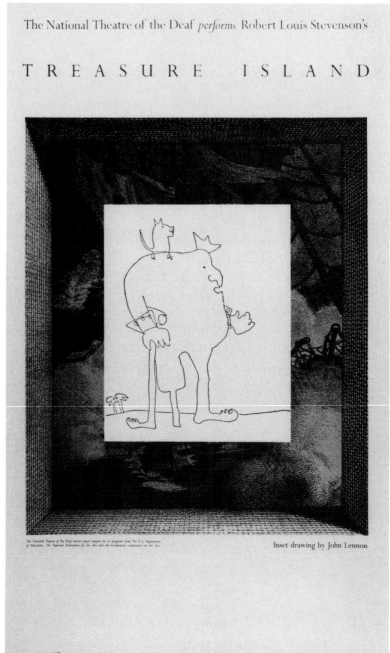

The National Theatre of the Deaf receives major support for its programs from The U.S. Department of Education, The National Endowment for the Arts and the Connecticut Commission on the Arts.

Inset drawing by John Lennon

They are a National Treasure. You Hear and See Every Word.

CHAPTER 3

The Traveling Troupe

The seventies were fruitful years for the young company. Each fall, the troupe set out on a nine-week tour, returning to their homes and families for a few weeks over the Christmas holidays, then back to Connecticut to prepare for another nine-week tour during the spring.

Being on the road twenty-six weeks annually, giving between sixty and seventy performances during each nine-week stint, was often grueling. Yet, for the love of their craft, the young actors left the security of their homes and families, many staying with the troupe for years.

On a typical tour, it was not unusual to work fourteen days, nonstop, with each performance expected to be as fresh as the first. Willy Conley, a veteran NTD player, has said that "one of the biggest challenges we faced on a long tour was to keep the show alive, night after night, as if we were performing it for the first time."[1]

Never knowing exactly what to expect at the next stop, the entourage learned to adapt to the conditions they faced along the way. Stages at every stop were different, ranging from proscenium to raised platforms, in every shape and size; unfamiliar

45

backstages with hazardous exits; and once, while performing in China, the stage was full of fleas![2]

On the road, the bus was home, and the other members of the troupe, family. The members set up housekeeping on the bus—tailoring their compartments to suit individual tastes and personalities. Seats were removed from the bus to allow for more room. Some kept pictures of the loved ones they so rarely saw taped to the windows; others kept flowers and books, while some preferred an ice chest serving as a table for card playing.[3]

Performance fees in the seventies ranged from $2,000 to $5,000, much less than the $4,000 to $9,000 they were commanding by the early nineties.

With schedules typically established six months to two years in advance, the group had to become highly organized—sending stage crews traveling with equipment, props, and costumes a couple of days ahead of the cast, and developing a smooth flow of communication among the different branches of the troupe. Because NTD had no home stage, the company, usually made up of nine deaf actors and two or three hearing actors, practiced productions in a rehearsal hall, the Rose Barn Theater at the O'Neill Center.

The constant travel puts a strain on relationships, so it has become a matter of practice for NTD to select either single people or married couples. The makeup of the group has become somewhat predictable, too, as there is usually a muscular male, such as Ed Waterstreet; an older gentleman, such as Andy Vasnick; and then a small, dark-haired actress, such as Linda Bove. There seems to be a tendency to select heavy-set actresses who lean toward the comical side, such as Mary Beth Miller, and typically, there is a medium-sized male, like Tim Scanlon, Willy Conley, or Adrian Blue. A close study of Appendix B, which lists NTD alumni, confirms this pattern of cast selection.

The hardships and obstacles never stood in the way of their artistic growth, and, indeed, the seventies were a significant time for creativity and experimentation.

Though the company performed mostly classical plays and original works, for the first time, they also did two original plays about deafness. A total of nineteen productions were presented between 1970 and 1979. (The repertoire, season by season, is listed in Appendix A.) Of those productions, two were major television presentations; five were adaptations of European classics; three were original pieces, two of which were about deaf culture; six were programs composed of whole poems or parts of poems, letters, essays, novels, and stories; and three were American plays.

The American works included Virgil Thomson and Gertrude Stein's *Four Saints in Three Acts,* an abstract opera; Dennis Scott's *Sir Gawain and the Green Knight,* based on Arthurian legend (commissioned by the Kennedy Center for the Performing Arts); and once again, one of the company staples, Wilder's *Our Town*—the play that had initially inspired Hays upon seeing it performed by the Gallaudet students in 1961—was performed before audiences in Japan, Korea, and Singapore.

Six other pieces included "Journeys" (from collected poems by Richard Lewis); *On the Harmfulness of Tobacco* by Chekhov, a satirical monologue by a henpecked college professor; *Children's Letters to God,* touching missives from children to God, collected by Eric Marshall and Stuart Hample; *Quite Early One Morning,* a popular narrative verse about a youth growing up in a Welsh town, by Dylan Thomas; and *The Wooden Boy* by David Hays, tailored after Collodi's *Pinocchio,* the story of a wooden boy with a moral message.

The five productions of classics were Buchner's bawdy play about morals and vices, *Woyzeck;* the Sumerian legend *Gilgamesh,* one of the world's oldest known legends—a story of a prince searching for the meaning of life and brotherhood; *The Three Musketeers,* the universally popular story about three fun-loving members of the French king's elite guard, by Alexandre Dumas père; Voltaire's satire about a youth's search for logic in a world of wars and confusion, *Optimism,* from his novel *Candide;* Ansky's classical Yiddish play about life, fear, evil, death, and justice, *The Dybbuk;* and Jonson's *Volpone,* a satirical English play with an Italian setting that traces the reaction of friends and relatives toward the "pretended" death of a miser.

Two major television presentations were made by NTD: *A Child's Christmas in Wales* by Dylan Thomas, narrated by Sir Michael Redgrave, became a CBS holiday favorite for several years; and *Who Knows One,* a WGBH-TV (Boston) special about Passover.

Two original company pieces, *My Third Eye* and *Parade,* depicted the comic and tragic lives of deaf people. *My Third Eye* (1971–72) was rife with satirical overtones and many role reversals between hearing and deaf characters. It marked the first time that deaf company members had assumed responsibility for directing and designing sets and costumes. The biographical, five-part play featured a collection of skits and profiles of deaf company members. Dorothy Miles codirected a piece entitled "Side Show" and Bernard Bragg directed "Manifest." Cheryl Conte, a 1970 graduate of Gallaudet, designed the costumes, and Alfredo Corrado, also from Gallaudet, designed the set. All in all, it took seven months to develop the play.[4]

One reviewer wrote that the play "might best be described as a bittersweet adventure, often depicting incidents that are at once joyous and defeating."[5] An excerpt, by Bernard Bragg, supports this observation.

> It took me weeks and weeks before I was able to make my "K" sound right. At the end of my first school year, there was a demonstration for the parents and visitors. I came up to the platform and made that one letter. The audience applauded, but my mother, who is deaf, just stared at me as if to ask, "Was that all you had learned during all that time?"[6]

Because the play showed the deaf experiences in the hearing world, *My Third Eye* was tremendously popular with deaf audiences. Miles's codirector, Joseph Chaikin, founder of the Open Theatre, however, was disappointed because he "was looking for a form—much more of a social protest."[7]

While the seventies rocked the nation with radical productions such as *Hair, Slave Ship,* and *Streamers,* NTD's repertoire remained conservative. Chaikin's disappointment with NTD can be understood in this light. Hays, however, was more interested in developing an art form than in presenting controversial plays. To Hays, developing sign language as an innovative artistic means of expression was a primary goal—more important than choice of repertoire, survival during difficult economic times, or the need to allow deaf actors to showcase their talents.[8]

My Third Eye exemplifies the difference between theater *of* the deaf and theater *for* the deaf. It became an academic issue when the productions of *My Third Eye* and *Parade* proved to be more popular with the deaf audience than with the hearing playgoers, who probably felt that those bona fide deaf works were sometimes too didactic or political.

The "deaf" plays did not bring in a significant number of hearing people. Typically, NTD's audiences were made up largely of hearing people, and they failed to identify with, or understand, deaf culture. It became obvious that performing for the deaf community alone would not support a touring professional theater for even one season. This cold reality particularly struck Bernard Bragg, who remembers "the sad truth that sank into me is that deaf audiences are simply too small a minority to sustain a thriving deaf professional theatre. To survive, plays about the deaf must be geared to hearing audiences by focusing on universal experiences and conflicts between the hearing and deaf worlds."[9]

One of the major goals of NTD in the seventies was to develop its own distinctive repertoire based on existing materials. According to David Hays, "My business is creating our own original works from nothing, so to speak. We just created totally original plays."[10]

According to Miles, "NTD had been creating original works from basic themes." The company has continued in that direction and moved toward a more physical form of theater. *Gilgamesh* (1972) and *Optimism* (1973) were created by company improvisation from themes selected by Hays and scripted by directors Larry Arrick (1972) and Hal Stone (1973). Both productions used a blend of old and new techniques, among them storytelling, cartoon sequences, mime, and music played by the actors.[11]

Fourteen of the works presented in the seventies were based on existing works. Five were based on plays and one opera, one each by Buchner, Ansky, Thomson and Stein, Scott, and Wilder. NTD treated even established plays as original pieces, since each needed to be translated into sign language. For example, *Four Saints in Three Acts,* as Hays noted, lent itself "wonderfully to transformation to sign language."[12]

> It's [the text's] words without the usual context. It is seen as sculpture, seen as things beautiful in themselves. And that worked beautifully in sign language. So that was another way of using sign language to develop the spoken texts that are not the usual dramatic texts.[13]

Priscilla, Princess of Power (1974–75) is based on a story written by famed New York cartoonist James Stevenson. According to one critic, NTD "breathes super-hilarious life into the supercharged world of Priscilla, where virtue is super sterling and vice is super odious."[14] In this production, the company explored the comic-book style by using balloon speech, frame pictures, and frozen motion.

Priscilla was the second original NTD play. *Priscilla, Princess of Power* was closer to theatricalized sign-language theater than deaf theater because the play did not intend to "portray deaf persons realistically and did not treat the subject of deafness, per se."[15]

The following year, *Parade* (1975–76) became the third original company piece. *Parade* was much like *My Third Eye* in that it depicted the deaf world more than the previous year's production had. The play was written by Jeff Wanshel and directed by Larry Arrick, who also directed several other NTD plays. Bernard Bragg, who also acted in the play, taught the stage signs.[16]

Though it was a modest, simple play, *Parade* received more consistent standing ovations than the company was accustomed to. Says Hays, "Sometimes it's the trick of a last line, a last image, that brings people to their feet—I don't know, but it was more popular than anything we had done at that point."[17]

As with *My Third Eye, Parade* used the psychological technique of role reversal: Deaf people became the majority and ruled, thereby turning the world inside out. The action was built around a montage of historical events, including a deaf Columbus, a deaf soap opera called "As the Hand Turns," and a deaf Superman.[18] This production was very popular with both deaf and hearing audiences.

During the seventies, NTD received numerous awards, perhaps the most important being the Tony Award for Theatrical Excellence in 1977. Also in that year, Gallaudet University bestowed an honorary doctorate on David Hays for his contributions to theater, education, and deafness throughout the United States and the world. The following year, NTD was awarded the Connecticut Commission on the Arts Award.

The growth and success of NTD were paralleled by gains in the American deaf community during the seventies. There was a surge of new programs for deaf students at the community-college level,[19] and in 1971, on the Gallaudet campus, a national demonstration school—Model Secondary School for the Deaf —designed to showcase innovative educational techniques, was established.

Eight major sign-language books were released during the seventies, more than during any other decade in history. Two books that contributed to dispelling myths about deaf people were also published: McCay Vernon and Edward Mindel wrote *They Grow in Silence* (1971), and Leo Jacobs followed with *A Deaf Adult Speaks Out* (1974).

Perhaps even more significantly, Congress passed Public Law 94-142, "The Education for All Handicapped Children Act," which opened the doors of public schools to all disabled children whose parents did not wish to send them to state residential schools. Because the Little Theatre of the Deaf catered largely to public schools, the passage of this new law significantly increased its bookings.

As the country began to move slowly toward acceptance of people with disabilities, the first real civil rights legislation for people with disabilities passed. Section 504 of the Rehabilitation Act of 1973 required that places receiving federal funds be accessible to all. And by the end of the decade, television had finally become accessible via decoders that revealed closed captions.

Demands for performances in regional and university theaters began cropping up across the country, greatly increasing the number of bookings for NTD. The company did more than half of its business with colleges and universities. Other bookings came from regional professional theaters and small community theaters.

Countercultural trends of the decade also encouraged the production of two mainstream plays that presented deaf people in major roles. In 1971, Robert Wilson, one of America's foremost avant-garde directors and storyboard playwrights, premiered *Deafman Glance.* Wilson developed his unconventional play out of his experiences with a young black deaf boy. Then in 1979, Mark Medoff penned the most famous story about deafness to date—*Children of a Lesser God.* This lyrical love story was written as a tribute to Phyllis Frelich, a former NTD player.

Frelich was propelled into the national spotlight with her remarkable portrayal of Sarah. The play, highly successful with hearing audiences, moved from New Mexico State University to the Mark Taper Forum in 1979, and later to New York, where it won three Tony awards for best play, best actress (Frelich), and best actor (John Rubinstein). *Children of a Lesser God* hired former NTD players, stage managers, and understudies as well.

Ten years later, the movie version of *Children of a Lesser God* was to be a showcase for another deaf actress, Marlee Matlin, who has gone on to blaze trails in Hollywood for actors who are deaf. Not only was Matlin the youngest person to ever win an

Academy Award for best actress, she was the first deaf person to win, making history as she laid claim to one of America's most coveted honors.

Children of a Lesser God made Hollywood and Broadway history for three reasons. First and foremost was that a deaf actress had the leading role, not a hearing person such as Jane Wyman in *Johnny Belinda* or Amy Irving in *Voices*. Secondly, sign language was given sincere exposure, and the beauty of the language was demonstrated for artistic and cinematic interest. Lastly, certain issues related to deafness were explored with a limited, though adequate, point of view; there were no disparaging, condescending, or otherwise negative attitudes toward deafness and deaf people.

Had *Children of a Lesser God* carried a stronger deaf point of view with a hammering didactic style and more deaf characters, the hearing world might not have so readily accepted this story or its message. Indeed, deaf actors and actresses in America were finally gaining the respect they deserved. NTD, time and again, would be the springboard from which those talents emerged.

During this same period, Sheldon Altfeld, a respected producer from Hollywood with no background in deafness, sign language, or deaf theater, saw a signed version of *Equus*. The play, directed by a hearing woman, Sue Wolf, featured an all-deaf cast, most of whom were from California State University, Northridge (CSUN). Altfeld became so enchanted with the beauty and significance of sign language that he decided he, too, would produce *Equus* with a deaf cast.

Using most of the original CSUN cast, Altfeld set up a theater company in Los Angeles called the West Coast Performing Arts Center for the Deaf. *Equus* ran for about six weeks in Hollywood's Pan Andreas Theatre, and when it completed its run, Altfeld went on to establish the first television network for deaf people—the Silent Network.

Among his small but talented crew, a number of former NTD

members could be found, including Julianna Fjeld, Ed Waterstreet, Lewis Merkin, Julianne Gold, Linda Bove, and Lou Fant.

Having worked with actors for many years, Altfeld saw one primary trait in the NTD alumni: "Although all of them were extremely good actors, they had one characteristic that other deaf actors did not have—discipline. They knew how to temper their egos and to focus on their roles. That's something that even seasoned hearing actors have trouble with."[20]

Over the years, many of the young actors who worked on the Silent Network attended the NTD Summer School (see chap. 5), and Altfeld has said that they "always came back with more skill and discipline."[21] The Silent Network also became a training ground for deaf producers, such as David Butterfield and David Pierce, the first two known deaf people to produce a variety of educational television programming for children and adults on a national scale.

Shanny Mow made his debut as a rising playwright in the 1970s. Mow, a 1961 graduate of Gallaudet, is considered by many to be one of America's most outstanding deaf playwrights. He is a serious writer with a mischievous sense of humor. Mow has lent his many talents over a period of about nine years to NTD and LTD—acting, writing, directing the summer Playwrights Conference, and serving as playwright-in-residence.

Mow holds the distinction of being the only deaf person to have had a play produced by NTD and is considered by many to be a "model for budding playwrights."[22] Using deafness as an artistic subtopic in two NTD plays that also contained universal themes, Mow was able to appeal to the majority of ticket buyers.

When he penned "How Do You Dance Without Music?" (1969), a witty essay that vividly portrays life in the day of a deaf man, his reputation was greatly enhanced as a writer. "How Do You Dance Without Music?" has appeared in a wide spectrum of publications, ranging from Leo Jacobs's *A Deaf Adult Speaks Out* (1974) to *Hearing Health* (formerly *The Voice*) magazine (1991).

As the country rolled into the eighties, NTD was gaining momentum and recognition in theater circuits. The original goals had been far surpassed, and the troupe, now experienced and having weathered a few storms, was positioned for new and unknown seas.

NOTES

1. Willy Conley, "Day 57: On the Road With the National Theatre of the Deaf," *Uncharted* (Fall 1990): 7–8.
2. Shanny Mow, letter to author, February 20, 1992.
3. Conley, 6.
4. Dorothy Miles, "A History of Theatre Activities in the Deaf Community of the United States," Master's thesis, Connecticut College, 1974, 62.
5. John M. Heidger, "The History of the Deaf in America: The Silent Stage," Master's thesis, Southern Illinois University, 1979, 35.
6. Jack Gannon, *Deaf Heritage: A Narrative History of Deaf America* (Silver Spring, Md.: National Association of the Deaf, 1981), 355.
7. David Hays, interview with author, March 10, 1988.
8. Hays interview.
9. Bernard Bragg, *Lessons in Laughter: The Autobiography of a Deaf Actor* (Washington, D.C.: Gallaudet University Press, 1989), 193.
10. Hays interview.
11. Miles, 63.
12. David Hays, taped interview, June 20, 1992.
13. Hays interview, March 1988.
14. *NTD Spotlight* (Winter 1975), 7.
15. Heidger, 38.
16. NTD playbill, *Parade,* November 21, 1975, 2.
17. Hays interview, June 1992.
18. Heidger, 39.
19. Gannon, xxx to xxxl.

20. Sheldon Altfeld, letter to author, April 21, 1992.

21. Ibid.

22. John V. Van Cleve, ed., *Gallaudet Encyclopedia of Deaf People and Deafness,* s.v. "Writers in Literature," by Robert Panara (New York: McGraw-Hill, 1987), 192.

CHAPTER 4

At Home and Abroad

*O*ver a span of twenty-five years, NTD has completed more than fifty touring seasons, something no other American professional touring acting company has done. And when the company toured its fiftieth state in 1980–81, it became the first touring company to accomplish this feat. Overall, NTD has presented more than 6,000 performances in America.

More than twenty-five different productions were performed by NTD between 1980 and 1993 in tours across the United States. The repertoire during this decade consisted of established poems, stories, novels, essays, and a film; two recycled classical works from the previous decade; two American plays; four original NTD plays; three television presentations; and five local holiday performances. (See Appendix A for a season-by-season listing of the repertoire.)

Between 1980 and 1983, Shanny Mow wrote three original NTD plays. The first, an athletic spoof entitled *The Iliad, Play by Play* (1980), based on Homer's epic, used a Super Bowl football game as a metaphor about armies battling each other in a light-hearted way. Ed Waterstreet staged the play, making him the third deaf director of an NTD production. Dorothy Miles and Bernard Bragg were the first two.) *The Iliad* marked the first time NTD used the combined talents of a deaf writer and a deaf director for a production.

Mow's second play was a western spoof in Kabuki style, *The Ghost of Chastity Past, or the Incident at Sashimi Junction* (1981). Directed by Peter Sellars, the play was set in a western town and included a gunfight, but the actors wore Japanese costumes.

Mow then teamed with Hays, and together they wrote *Parzival: From the Horse's Mouth* (1982), a comedy based on the English legend of the Holy Grail and presented with colorful Arthurian costumes. In some ways, it treated the theme of deaf people searching for their own Holy Grail; in other words, the search for acceptance by their hearing parents.

The remaining sixteen productions of the eighties were a mix of serious and festive works. The two "revived" works were *Gilgamesh* (first staged in 1972 and restaged in 1981); and *The Dybbuk* (1974 and 1987–88). When both plays were originally performed, the critics and the audiences had reacted favorably.[1] Hays does not like to compare different productions of the same play, but when the same play has been produced more than once, it is probably because of its past artistic and commercial success. Hays recalls that in restaging *The Dybbuk*

> Chuck Baird [deaf designer and actor] did a beautiful job on the sets. The European village costumes [by Fred Voelpel] were similar. There is a conscious memory that they had been a little bit tight perhaps. So we loosened them up ... a little more air in them. There was a scheme on the lighting which we did not have before. We had great performers last night [March 9, 1988]; we had great performers before.[2]

In 1984, NTD was one of four American companies invited to perform at the Olympic Arts Festival in Los Angeles during the company's thirty-fifth United States tour. Robert Fitzpatrick, director of the 1984 Olympic Arts Festival, stated that NTD had been chosen for "its pursuit of excellence which is comparable to that which world class athletes display at the Olympic Games."[3]

Hays chose to perform *The Hero with a Thousand Faces* for the festival. According to the Olympic Arts Festival program, this play is based on the landmark mythology book by Joseph Campbell and adapted by director Larry Arrick; the production weaves together several of the world's fanciful fairy tales, legends, and myths.[4]

Throughout the eighties, NTD continued to present established poems, stories, and novels. Dylan Thomas was the poet of choice. Six of his works were performed between 1967 and 1989, including *Songs from Milk Wood, A Child's Christmas in Wales,* and *Quite Early One Morning.* When asked about his frequent use of Thomas's poems, Hays responded,

> We always feel at home with Dylan Thomas. We did it because I love it. *A Child's Christmas in Wales* was intended for radio; a play for voices. When we stage these pieces, there isn't any directional commenting on set characters are doing this and that. It is just speech. So very often when they are produced, that aspect is very arbitrary. You can move around, you have many things to do. So our way of putting speech on the hands, putting speech in the air gives you so much life and color to the words that you don't need anything else if you don't want to. And this principle is very important to the Company.[5]

Hays and company sought visual equivalents of the images and sounds of poems by Thomas and others.

Three American works became important plays for NTD during the eighties. *All the Way Home,* adapted for the stage by Tad Mosel from James Agee's novel *A Death in the Family,* was directed by the late Colleen Dewhurst in 1984. David Hays had been the set designer for this 1961 Pulitzer Prize–winning play when it was produced in New York with Miss Dewhurst in a leading role. At NTD, Mosel's play was designed by Chuck

Baird, the second deaf designer in NTD's history; the sign master was Shanny Mow.[6] This play represents a rare instance when
NTD did a straight play with little alteration.

Perhaps because Mosel's adaptation[7] had been successful,
the adaptation of another novel was selected by NTD for its 1986
production: *The Heart Is a Lonely Hunter* by Carson McCullers.
(Alan Arkin, a member of NTD's artistic board, had earned an
Oscar nomination for his performance in the leading role in the
1969 film version.) With this production, NTD ventured into a
new area—for the first time, the company staged a play that
included a deaf character, John Singer. Although he is not
viewed by the deaf community as a typical deaf person, Singer
is "neither ignorant nor grotesque."[8]

The third adaptation of an American work was *Farewell, My
Lovely,* based on E. B. White's essay about the Model T Ford. An
authentic Model T was actually assembled and later dismantled
every night during this production. This 1986 play was the second part of a double bill, which included Ryunosuke Akutagawa's melodramatic Japanese murder tale, *In a Grove,* directed
by Arvin Brown.

For the 1988–89 national tour, *The King of Hearts* became
NTD's first work adapted from a film. For this, NTD developed
its own script from the 1967 film classic. The story

> is an enchanted idyll of mythic proportions set during World War I
> in a French town booby-trapped by the German army. An allied sol-
> dier, drafted to find the bombs, doesn't realize that the town's citi-
> zens, everyone from the bishop to the madam, are really the light-
> hearted and lightheaded inhabitants who have escaped from the
> local loony bin. By the time he learns the truth, he's been charmed
> by these endearing clowns who crown him their "king of hearts"
> and he has found love, madness, and sanity—all in one day.[9]

J Ranelli, who directed many of NTD's most successful productions in collaboration with the company, adapted the story
from the film. Hays commented that "the difficult contemporary
work [film] is totally cinematic in conception. We're going to

Anne Bancroft on the movie set of *The Miracle Worker* in 1962. Bancroft became interested in developing a troupe of deaf actors when she began studying for the role of Anne Sullivan in the stage production of *The Miracle Worker*. PHOTO COURTESY OF THE ACADEMY OF MOTION PICTURE ARTS AND SCIENCES

Edna S. Levine, a psychologist and professor at the New York University Deafness Research and Training Center, was an influential proponent of a professional theater group of deaf actors. PHOTO COURTESY OF GALLAUDET UNIVERSITY ARCHIVES

Members of the Washington, D.C., area Deaf community celebrated the birth of NTD in April 1967 with a special party. Pictured here about to cut the cake are (*left to right*) Robert Sanderson, president of the National Association of the Deaf; David Hays, artistic director of NTD; Boyce Williams, chief of the U.S. Office of Vocational Rehabilitation; and Douglas Burke, director of the NAD Cultural Program.

George C. White, president of the Eugene O'Neill Center, stands near the Rose Barn Theater in Waterford, Connecticut, in 1966. White provided the first home for NTD. PHOTO COURTESY OF THE O'NEILL CENTER ARCHIVES

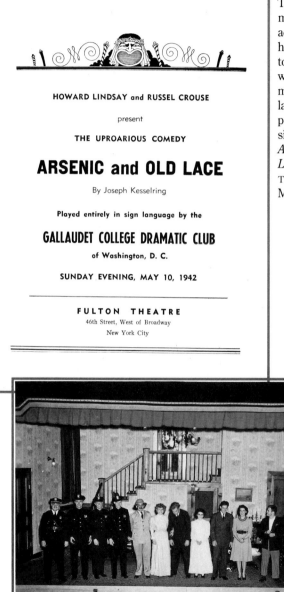

HOWARD LINDSAY and RUSSEL CROUSE

present

THE UPROARIOUS COMEDY

ARSENIC and OLD LACE

By Joseph Kesselring

Played entirely in sign language by the

GALLAUDET COLLEGE DRAMATIC CLUB
of Washington, D. C.

SUNDAY EVENING, MAY 10, 1942

FULTON THEATRE
46th Street, West of Broadway
New York City

The first performance by deaf actors before a hearing audience took place in 1942 when the Dramatic Club of Gallaudet College presented a signed version of *Arsenic and Old Lace*. PHOTO COURTESY OF RICHARD MULLINS

Before their legendary New York appearance, the Gallaudet Dramatic Club performed *Arsenic and Old Lace* in Chapel Hall at Gallaudet College. PHOTO COURTESY OF RICHARD MULLINS

Pictured here are three of the seventeen original NTD company members who joined in 1967. Bernard Bragg (*top left*), a successful actor and mime, helped David Hays recruit many fine deaf actors during the early years. Phyllis Frelich (*top right*) remained with the company for twelve years before leaving to pursue other acting opportunities. She won the 1980 Tony award for Best Actress for her performance as Sarah in *Children of a Lesser God.* Andy Vasnick (*bottom*) also stayed with NTD for twelve years as an actor and administrator. PHOTOS COURTESY OF NTD

Mary Beth Miller (*top left*) became an author, storyteller, and comedienne. Tim Scanlon (*top right*), a versatile actor, performed for a total of six years with NTD. Will Rhys (*bottom*) spent two years with NTD. He later returned to direct several NTD productions in the early 1990s, and in May 1993 he became the artistic director. PHOTOS COURTESY OF NTD

My Third Eye became NTD's first play with a genuine deaf point of view (*left to right*: Carol Fleming, Pat Graybill, Bernard Bragg, and Richard Kendall).
Photo courtesy of NTD

The company strikes a pose in *My Third Eye* during the 1971–1972 tour season.
PHOTO BY JAY AARE, COURTESY OF NTD

Howard Seago (*second from left*) starred in the second *Gilgamesh* production in 1981. The bamboo sticks became a popular NTD stage property that afforded countless creative uses. PHOTO COURTESY OF NTD

NTD has staged two successful productions of *The Dybbuk*–the first in 1974 (*pictured above*) and the second in 1987. PHOTO COURTESY OF NTD

Linda Bove starred in *Priscilla, Princess of Power* during the 1974–1975 season. PHOTO COURTESY OF NTD

Tim Scanlon starred as Pinocchio in *The Wooden Boy* by David Hays. The play's underlying theme used deafness as an analogy to Pinocchio's woodenness. PHOTO COURTESY OF NTD

Nat Wilson signs BUTTERFLY to Mike Josephson in *All the Way Home,* one of the few straight American plays produced by NTD. PHOTO BY DAVID HAYS, COURTESY OF NTD

Four actors engage in a conversation in *Farewell My Lovely*. Like all NTD stage props, the Model T Ford was easy to pack and assemble (*left to right*: Charles Struppmann, Chuck Baird, Charles Hornet, and Andy Vasnick). PHOTO BY DAVID HAYS, COURTESY OF NTD

Shhh! *Parade* was one of the two NTD productions that had a deaf theme. Photo by David Hays, courtesy of NTD

transform it into a play . . . right from scratch. It is not like doing a text like *The Dybbuk.* "[10] This was also NTD's first comedy since Mow and Hays's *Parzival* (1982).

The company's American television specials during the eighties were composed of poems as narrated by Jason Robards (1980) and Chita Rivera (1981). Robards narrated Robert Frost's "The Silken Tent," and Rivera narrated García Lorca's "Road to Cordoba." Tessuko Kuroyanagi narrated another production about a Japanese poet, Issa, in 1981. These NTD productions were part of the series "Festival of Hands."

Between 1983 and 1988, NTD also presented five Christmas productions in Connecticut. Besides the NTD tradition of performing Dylan Thomas's *A Child's Christmas in Wales,* the company also presented *Race a Comet, Catch a Tale* (1985) and *Gift of the Magi* (1986).

All of NTD's plays after 1982 were developed in Chester, Connecticut, a small rustic town located twenty minutes from Waterford. Irving Stark, a successful New York businessman, donated money to buy the land, a mill, and a house in memory of his wife, Hazel, who had loved the performing arts and had been concerned about the education and well-being of people with disabilities. Only a year earlier, NTD had become an independent not-for-profit organization by disassociating itself from the O'Neill Center. When asked about the reasons for breaking away from the O'Neill Center after thirteen years in Waterford, Hays said it was because of "poor financial management there.[11] When the Reagan administration began, and we saw the cutbacks that were coming in, we felt we could no longer afford to live with the big cut the O'Neill Center was taking. There was not enough value returned for the money."[12]

Hays later added that the new location gave the company "increased energy, artistic energy, quality of work . . . and managing our own resources, time, and money."[13]

George C. White, president of the Eugene O'Neill Theatre Center, realized that NTD had outgrown the facilities and services of the center, and that the center could no longer meet the needs required by the growing company. And because NTD desired autonomous control of its budget, it made sense that NTD depart from the O'Neill Center and establish itself as a separate not-for-profit corporation.[14]

During the eighties, major theatrical awards, including Hays's second honorary degree—from Wesleyan University in 1986—gave NTD more recognition and prestige. Perhaps equally important was the Centennial Award, presented by the National Association of the Deaf (NAD) in 1980. The NAD citation read:

> In honoring the National Theatre of the Deaf with its Centennial Award (1980), the NAD recognizes a company which has, within a short span of years, added a new dimension to communication receptivity and created an enriched appreciation of capabilities and talents of deaf people throughout the world.[15]

The National Association of the Deaf honored the NTD again in 1984 for its continued success.

For the 1989–90 touring season, *One More Spring,* based on a novel by Robert Nathan and written and directed by J Ranelli, became another traditional kind of production. Based on a simple story line with a strong narrative style, the play made use of numerous images to concur with the romantic theme. Interestingly, the following season resulted in yet another play based on an established novel.

Treasure Island (1991–92), a warm family-oriented story by Robert Louis Stevenson appealed to deaf and hearing audiences alike. According to Julianna Fjeld, both deaf and hearing children were seen having imaginary sword fights after each production throughout the touring season.

Yet another honor, the 1992 Media Award, was given to NTD in June 1992 by the Deafness Research Foundation. The distinguished Media Award recognized NTD for its "worldwide artistic and theatrical contributions."[16]

While building and consolidating its American reputation, NTD was also becoming an international force, and by 1992 had toured in thirty-two countries, nearly twice the number of any other American theater company.[17] (See Appendix E for a listing of foreign tours.)

In 1969, NTD presented its first European performance, which took place in the Teatro Sistino in Rome. The home of improvised commedia dell'arte, Italy was quick to welcome the American performers. In Rome, two newspapers offered interesting reviews of the double bill composed of *Songs from Milk Wood* and *Sganarelle. Il Giorano* stated, "It is obvious that, to understand what inestimable value words have, it is necessary to be prisoners, like these angels of silence."[18] *L'Unita* echoed much the same idea: "[The word] relived by the gesture which rediscovers its most profound dimensions on words that destroy itself and renews itself into a more 'sonorous' language, then we discover suddenly our organic muteness."[19]

Italian critics, along with most of their European colleagues, seemed to enjoy the NTD performances, perhaps because Europe has always been a multilingual and multicultural region that tolerates formal and informal nonverbal communication modes.

When NTD first toured Europe in 1969, only Russia, among the European countries, had a deaf theater group. Known as the Moscow Theatre of Mimicry and Gesture, it was the first modern deaf professional theater with a full-time company. It was founded in 1917, subsequently disbanded, then revived during the 1940s, and finally professionalized in 1962. However, this group had never toured in Western Europe, thus giving NTD the honor of being the first deaf theater group to tour there.

Company members first saw deaf Russians perform during the summer of 1969 when, after touring England, France, Israel, Italy, and Yugoslavia that spring and summer, NTD and the Russians participated in the Deaf Festival held in Belgrade in conjunction with the World Games for the Deaf. The festival included mime, dance, and theater groups. Hays subsequently visited Russia and made these comments about the deaf theater there:

> They had a staff of about 110 when I visited there in 1969. I went to Russia and saw them in 1970, and they were very, very well trained. They train all day and they train for many years. Their signing, of all the shows I ever saw, was quite vestigial, not large. They didn't make that the art form. They signed, they mouthed the words, speakers sitting in the front row with microphones watched their lips and put words in them. So it was like lip-sync. They had a little orchestra, smallish. So it kind of reduced it to puppetry. It made them all look like actors who had simply memorized something instead of actors who had a sense of choice. It was the opposite of what we [NTD] wanted, and not trying to imitate another's play.[20]

Hays's observations coincide with those of a deaf Bulgarian who had witnessed a deaf Russian performance more than ten years earlier. The Bulgarian wrote,

> In these performances the usual speech of the deaf is used together with their peculiar manner of talking and understanding one another. Thus, they use on the stage vocal speech, the one-hand alphabet, and the common mimicry. In front of the stage stands an interpreter, who interprets on the microphone the meaning of the conversation held on the stage between the deaf actors.[21]

Both observations made the Moscow Theatre of Mimicry and Gesture appear mechanical, but one must remember that the government controlled theater policies in those times, and strict oralism and fingerspelling were the official teaching methods in Russia.

In 1973 and 1975, before "détente" and "glasnost" had become fashionable, NTD and the Moscow Theatre exchanged actors. Bernard Bragg spent four weeks in Moscow, where he played the role of Hermes in *Prometheus Bound.*[22] According to *Soviet Life* in 1975, [Ira] Frederick Aldridge, the famed black American actor, had been the last American to perform with a

Soviet company prior to this time.[23] Then Michael Slipchenko, a famous Russian deaf actor, performed the role of Sender in the NTD production of *The Dybbuk* in 1975. Slipchenko had become deaf at the age of six from scarlet fever.[24]

Between 1965 and 1985, NTD invited members from five other foreign amateur or professional deaf theaters either to tour with NTD or to attend its annual Professional School for Deaf Theatre Personnel. Among these were members of Denmark's Doves Teater (established in 1960) who later attended the NTD summer school. Also included were Jean St. Clair, Pat Keysell, and several English performers from the English Interim Theatre (established in 1968) who attended the summer program several times.

Gunilla Wagstrom was sent to the Tyst Teater (Silent Theatre) of Sweden to study and perform with NTD in 1973 and 1974. Wagstrom, like Dorothy Miles, was multitalented, showing a proclivity for directing, writing plays, acting, and business management. After several performers from Tyst Teater attended NTD in the summer of 1977, the Swedish group became fully professional for the first time since its founding as an amateur theater in 1972.

In turn, the NTD learned from the Europeans. In 1972, NTD accepted an invitation to spend three weeks, May 6–27, with Peter Brook and the International Center for Theatre Research in Paris. Brook, well known for his innovative theater work, was then especially noted for his production of *Marat/Sade* (1964), a blend of Artaudian methods and Brechtian techniques, and *A Midsummer Night's Dream* (1970) at England's Royal Shakespeare Company. His Parisian center was founded in 1971 to explore communication that transcends linguistic barriers. Brook invited the NTD to Paris because he wanted to work "with actors who use the language of sign as a theatrical medium."[25]

During their stay at the center, NTD developed skills in the use of bamboo poles, which have since been incorporated in some productions. The poles are used as weapons, houses, tools, carriers, and noisemakers.

The question has been raised as to whether the Parisian encounter motivated NTD to produce *Gilgamesh* during the following season, since the play epitomized many of the concepts developed in Brook's workshop. Hays responds,

> No. That type of theater was very much in fashion, you couldn't avoid it . . . and it had some of that flavor. Before we went to Peter, we'd prepared and done a production called *My Third Eye* (1971–72). Working with Peter didn't create that kind of style with us as much as our work before we worked with Peter. But he gave us a lot of confidence, made us trust ourselves. That was the great thing. We felt proud of our style of acting.[26]

Thus, NTD's own experiences were apparently reinforced by its work at the International Center for Theatre Research. Whatever its inspiration, *Gilgamesh* (1981) became one of NTD's most successful productions.

Several former NTD company members have influenced deaf theater in other countries. In January of 1976, Jane Wilk, Alfredo Corrado, and Julianna Fjeld traveled to France to help establish the International Visual Theatre. Corrado has remained in Paris ever since that first visit. The company has also played an influential role in the establishment of other theaters in France, England, Australia, Canada, India, Japan, and China. Members of Canada's Theatre Visuel des Sourds (1986) and Show of Hands (1980) interned at NTD. The Australia Theatre of the Deaf was formed in 1974 after the first NTD tour there; in 1978, it became fully professional under the management of two NTD alumni, Carol Lee Aquiline and Ben Stout. Since 1974, a good number of Australians have attended the NTD summer school.

The influence of NTD has also been felt in India. In 1986, four Indians attended the nineteenth annual Professional School for Theatre Personnel, and in July of 1987, NTD sent Mike Lamitola to conduct workshops to help India establish a pantomime group.

The first tour to the Far East during the 1979–80 season established strong ties with Japan, South Korea, and Singapore. The Korean Deaf Theatre, which had performed rather sporadically from 1940 to 1973, presented NTD with a plaque in 1979.[27] When Hays visited Japan in 1960 and 1970 as an adviser and designer, he developed a friendship with one of Japan's most popular performers, Tetsuko Kuroyanagi, who publicized NTD's 1979 tour so successfully that it was treated as a major event. As a result of her efforts, the Crown Prince, who became Emperor Akihito in 1989, and Princess of Japan went backstage to meet the company. The enormous support and enthusiasm aroused at that time led to the formation of the Japanese Theatre of the Deaf (JTD) in April 1980. Furthermore, two deaf actors, Izaki Tetsuya and Akihiro Yonaiyama, toured with NTD in America in 1981–82 and again in 1986–87. Yonaiyama eventually became the artistic director of the Japanese Theatre of the Deaf. In August of 1988, NTD teamed up with Japan's National Theatre of the Deaf and other foreign deaf individuals from China and India at the first International Tokyo Theatre Festival to present Akutagawa's *In a Grove.*[28]

Several groups were involved in the diplomatic and cultural planning for NTD's visit: among them, the Chinese Dramatists' Association, the Beijing Film Academy, Columbia University's Center for United States–China Arts Exchange, and the China Institute at California State University at Northridge. However, even with all this diplomatic activity, the historic tour would not have materialized had support not been forthcoming from the Max Factor Family and the Henry Luce Foundations, whose grants funded most of the tour.

In 1992 Venezuela, Northern Ireland, and South Africa became the thirtieth, thirty-first, and thirty-second countries visited in twenty-eight foreign tours, thus expanding NTD's international reputation to five continents.

NTD was also responsible, directly or indirectly, for the establishment of eighteen amateur and professional theaters of or for the deaf in the United States and overseas. During this decade, the first professional deaf American directors, playwrights, designers, and theater administrators also began to make their mark; most had been trained by NTD.

Long before the United Nations declared the eighties to be the Decade of the Disabled, NTD had been breaking ground for people who were deaf and people who were disabled. NTD was undertaking innovative experiments in sign language as an artistic medium, converting poems and other nondramatic sources into "sculptures in the air" and working with foreign actors.

From 1970 to 1992, NTD toured extensively and successfully both in the United States and abroad, and had earned the distinction of being the foremost deaf theater company in the world.

Indeed, this proud showboat of the nation's deaf actors had met the challenges of the rough seas of the entertainment world, sailing magnificently at times and struggling at others. Ports around the world had been visited and charmed by her beauty. She sailed on.

NOTES

1. David Hays, interview with author, March 10, 1988.
2. Hays interview.
3. NTD Olympic issue, 1984, 1.
4. Ibid.
5. Hays interview.
6. NTD Program Book, 1985.
7. Steve Baldwin, personal notes, March 1985.
8. Trent Batson and Eugene Bergman, eds., *Angels and Outcasts: An Anthology of Deaf Characters in Literature,* 3rd ed. (Washington, D.C.: Gallaudet University Press, 1985), 138.
9. "Tony Award-Winning NTD to Present King of Hearts [*sic*] During 1988–89 National Tour," *Silent News* (May 1988): 34.

10. Hays interview.

11. David Hays, interview with author, March 20, 1992.

12. Hays interview, March 1988.

13. David Hays, taped interview, June 20, 1992.

14. George White, letter to author, June 22, 1992.

15. NTD Tour Brochure, 1981–82.

16. Deafness Research Foundation News Release, May 1992.

17. NTD Program Book, "Twenty-Five Years," 1992.

18. George McClendon, "The Unique Contributions of the National Theatre of the Deaf to the American Theatre," Master's thesis, Catholic University, 1972, 80.

19. McClendon, 80.

20. Hays interview, March 1988.

21. Marcho Rudulov, "The Pantomime as a Salutary Source for the Intellectual, Moral and Artistic Development of the Deaf," unpublished paper, 1961 (Washington, D.C.: Gallaudet University Archives).

22. Robert Panara and John Panara, *Great Deaf Americans* (Silver Springs, Md.: T.J. Publishers, 1982), 107.

23. Panara and Panara, 107.

24. *NTD Spotlight* (Winter 1975): 6.

25. *NTD Spotlight* (Spring 1972): 3.

26. Hays interview, March 1988.

27. John V. Van Cleve, ed., *Gallaudet Encyclopedia of Deaf People and Deafness,* s.v. "National Theaters of the Deaf," by Shanny Mow (New York: McGraw-Hill, 1987), 232.

28. Roddy O'Connor, phone interview, July 26, 1988.

The Little Theatre of the Deaf

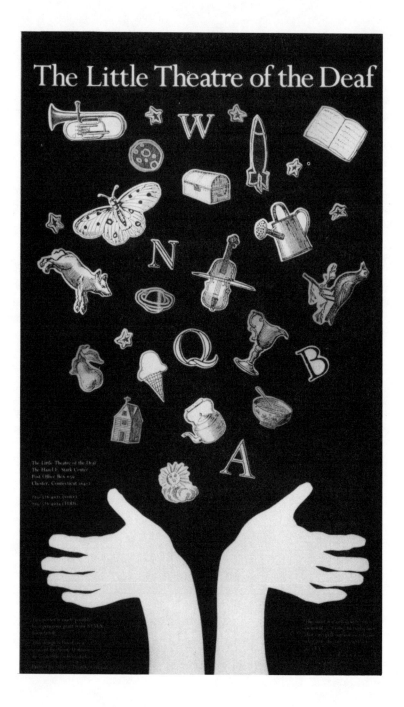

CHAPTER 5

Expanding the Scope of NTD

Several worthy programs have flourished during NTD's history. When the original grant was written in the sixties, the authors had no way of knowing just how successfully their goals would be met—and surpassed. While the company had far exceeded its primary goal of establishing a theater of the deaf, ten programs were also founded to further strengthen deaf theater, community relations, and the people who would continue to fuel its success.

Thus, NTD has served as a versatile touring company, one that can attribute at least some of its tremendous success to its wide range of activities for both the public and company members. This broad spectrum of programs includes activities in advocacy, the arts, and continued professional development of the NTD members.

Starting with the summer of 1967, before the troupe launched its first tour, a theater-training center for performers was established. Known as the Professional School for Deaf Theatre Personnel, sometimes called the NTD Summer School, Professional Theatre School, or Professional School, the program has garnered much goodwill throughout the years because NTD has always invited performers, drama teachers, and leaders of community theaters from across the country and overseas. Company members attend advanced classes, direct works-in-progress, and share their talents with the school participants.

Competition to participate in the training-intensive professional school is fierce, with only twenty people selected out of approximately two hundred applicants annually.[1] Once chosen, the lucky few are given a four- or five-week scholarship, which comes solely from funding by the U.S. Department of Education. Occasionally, hearing applicants are admitted—by invitation only. Applicants are selected on the basis of theater experience, potential as performers, and references from two theater people. Because of NTD's missionary goal of nourishing foreign theaters of the deaf, foreign applicants have been invited for the last two decades. Thus, in a sense, the school is an international one. When Japan's Theatre of the Deaf initiated its First Annual Summer Theatre Seminar in Tokyo in 1981, Andrew Vasnick, Michael Posnick, and Ed Waterstreet were invited to serve as instructors.[2]

The professional school schedule is a grueling one. Six days a week, the day begins at 7:30 A.M. and ends after 9:00 P.M. Only Mondays are free. Experts provide instruction in theater history, dance (modern, ballet, or Oriental), fencing, movement, improvisation, creative signing, stage and television acting, resource art work, creative writing, stage techniques, clowning, storytelling, theater management, play analysis, and morning calisthenics or tai chi. Then at 8:00 P.M., the students are treated to a special lecture in theater history or creative sign language; a silent movie or English-subtitled foreign movies; or a staged reading for one of the deaf or hearing playwrights.

Students are given assignments from some of the classes and are expected to perform individually or in groups. The workshops, classes, lectures, seminars, movies, performances, and meetings are tightly scheduled to ensure maximum participation and experimentation. Since its beginning in 1967, NTD has not had a single dropout from its professional school.[3]

An informal survey conducted by this author on the 1986 class of the professional school indicated that of the fifteen students in the first-year group, the median age was 27.5. All except three were college-educated. Each aspired to act, teach, or work in theater. Three participants preferred to teach either dance or work as wardrobe mistresses. Five participants expressed serious intentions of joining a hearing acting company, something that would have been unimaginable in 1966. At the end of the program, NTD hired three of the fifteen participants, two as company actors and one as a wardrobe mistress.

Although NTD sometimes recruits summer-school students as possible new members of the company, Andrew Vasnick, longtime (now former) administrator/director of the professional school, frequently reminded the students that they had not been invited there as a form of audition.[4] In 1986, Camille Jeter was one of the disappointed deaf actresses who had dreamed of becoming an NTD actress since she was twelve.[5] After spending three years with the Sunshine Company of Rochester, New York, she had hoped to be hired. Her disappointment was short-lived, however, for within a year, she was hired as an actress with the Little Theatre of the Deaf (LTD), and subsequently, with the NTD.

Jeter was one of the seven professional performers invited to participate in the "advanced students" group. Among the seven were three well-known professional deaf performers: Marlee Matlin, who at the time was an Oscar nominee for her portrayal of Sarah in *Children of a Lesser God;* Lewis Merkin, the original Orin of the Broadway play, *Children of a Lesser God,* and who had acted in many hearing plays as well; and Bobbie Beth Scoggins, a well-known freelance actress who has performed for both hearing and deaf theaters. The advanced students, joined by the current company members, have a schedule that includes acting, movement, directing, and writing. During the summer of 1986, Scoggins and Merkin accepted invitations to join LTD and NTD, respectively.

The third group of the 1986 professional school was made up entirely of foreigners, who mingled freely with their American counterparts. The average age of this group was twenty-eight. Of the ten foreigners in 1986, three were from India; three from Australia; two from Canada; and two from England. (One hearing observer from the Deaf India Theatre Company was already in the advanced group.) All either came at their own expense or with assistance from their own countries or theater groups. Their aspirations were similar to those of the Americans, except that some wanted to work with deaf children or youth.

The August 1988 issue of the *Silent News* indicates that three of the 1986 Professional School participants had become performers on the Silent Network.[6] Many of the Silent Network's performing crew had roots in the NTD professional school programs, either as students or instructors.[7]

Typical of many students who have expressed their appreciation to NTD, Mark Hoski of Washington State outlines the impact of the professional school on him in the summer of 1979 as follows:

- Assumed greater pride in working with professionals.
- Assumed a more professional outlook toward the various aspects of theatre.
- Am more capable of passing on learned techniques to others involved in theatre.
- Sustained greater personal confidence and knowledge of theatre and myself.
- Discovered more energy and creativity than I thought possible.
- Am more capable of assuming greater responsibility and weight in productions and performances.[8]

In order to meet the demand for a children's theater, NTD established the Little Theatre of the Deaf (LTD) in 1968, when the U.S. Office of Education awarded NTD a grant for a children's company.[9] In 1970, after the demand for the LTD's services had exceeded NTD's expectations, a second LTD group was formed. In 1972, it was one of the five American children's theater companies to perform at the ASSITEJ (International Association of Theatres for Children and Youth) Festival in Albany, New York.[10] Subsequently, LTD received another honor when the American Theatre Association presented it with the Jennie Heiden Award for excellence in professional children's theater. In 1977, LTD performed for the Theatres for Children Arts Festival at the Kennedy Center in Washington, D.C., in a specially commissioned play by Dennis Scott, *Sir Gawain and the Green Knight*. A third LTD was founded in 1978 especially to perform for inner-city schools, but due to lack of funding, the troupe was discontinued in 1978.

The Little Theatre of the Deaf is viewed by the NTD as an offshoot of the parent company. The two LTD companies currently spend about twenty-two weeks annually touring, giving about 125 performances (about twice the number of NTD performances), mostly in December, January, and May.[11] Made up of five actors and one stage manager, each troupe has one hearing and four deaf members. Occasionally, performers are hired to work with LTD on a contractual basis. The LTD performances last about fifty minutes and are usually given at public schools, and occasionally at museums, libraries, or parks. The following is a typical LTD program:

"Telling It Tall"—Tall tales and short stories to inspire and amuse
Sign Language Introduction by The Company, Directed by Adrian Blue
Ghost Story by The Company and Audience, Directed by Chuck Baird

Three Poems by e. e. cummings, Directed by David Hays
The Night the Bed Fell by James Thurber, Directed by Ed Water-
street
Your Game—Improvisation by The Company With the Audience,
Directed by Betty Beekman[12]

Each program introduces sign language and includes stories, poems, fairy tales, fables, or even radio plays. Young audiences are encouraged to use their own creativity and make suggestions for improvisations by the cast. The Little Theatre of the Deaf has gained international attention, performing in England, Europe, Japan, India, Hong Kong, Mexico, Venezuela, Trinidad, and China.

Helen Powers, a critic and early historian of NTD, once collected feedback from youngsters who had attended LTD performances. They reported that

- "The poems were most effective, you could almost feel them."
- "I myself have had cerebral palsy for eighteen years, and these two skits were a great inspiration to me."
- "Very expressive . . . almost like ballet."
- "Fantastically sensual."
- "I never realized that it was possible that feelings can be expressed so well by body movements."
- 'This presentation was so effective that at times I completely forgot that these persons were deaf."
- "Language of the hands seems to be a beautiful art form in itself."[13]

Much of the feedback from the young audiences and school educators over the last twenty-five years has been similar to that reported by Powers.

Before every LTD presentation, the sponsoring school district receives a study guide designed for a nondeaf audience. After each show, the LTD performers mingle freely with the youngsters to talk with them, answer questions, pose for pictures, and autograph LTD company photographs that are passed around the audience by the performers themselves. During the summers, LTD members appear on the Chester Village Green to tell stories to the public. Guest appearances on television's "Sesame Street" to tell stories led to Linda Bove's becoming a permanent resident as "Linda the Librarian" there, a post she has held since 1976.

Various publications have been produced by NTD in an effort to disseminate information about deaf performers—and to advocate their right to perform. Such publications include newsletters (*NTD Spotlight* and *Deaf Players' Guide*), booking brochures, and pamphlets. The *Deaf Players' Guide* was a listing that went to casting directors and other prospective employers. A grant that supported the *Actor's Advocate* newsletter was cut in 1983.[14] For several years, NTD used the grant to publish the *Deaf Players' Guide* (1978–83), which supported the cause of deaf actors throughout the country and the world. The following is a typical article, from a summer 1980 issue:

> What an exciting time to be working in the entertainment business! Who could have guessed that we would begin the 80's with a deaf actress winning the Tony award, a show about a deaf and hearing couple on Broadway, 5 or 6 TV projects featuring deaf performers, world-wide exchange of actors from various national theatres of the deaf, and approximately 35 community and professional theatres of the deaf performing in the United States.
>
> We now have access to interpreted performances, telecaption adaptor devices, deaf playwrights writing new works, grant money available from government and private resources for developing deaf arts projects and on and on.
>
> This means more work for us all and the possibility of real variety in our careers. It also means a growing responsibility for keeping our networks of communication open and offering real support to one another as we build and grow.

This newsletter is one way that we can share our resources and ideas. Keep the news and letters coming!

Elizabeth House, Actors' Advocate[15]

A few years earlier, NTD had joined other deaf advocacy groups, such as NAD, to secure roles for deaf actors that were going to hearing actors. A good example is the movie *Voices* (1979), starring Amy Irving, a hearing actress cast as a deaf character. This casting incited a nationwide protest led by NTD and others. The protest was only partially successful, and Irving kept the role. At least one career was derailed by such protests. In 1978, Audree Norton and her husband, Ken, became involved in a protest regarding the ABC After School Special "Mom and Dad Can't Hear Me." Audree and Ken had auditioned successfully for the roles of the deaf parents. And although the casting director had chosen them, he was overruled by the director, who preferred working with hearing actors. Audree filed a formal protest with the Screen Actors Guild branch office in San Francisco on the premise that no hearing performer had the right to play the role of a deaf character. The case was referred to the Los Angeles headquarters, but the director's decision was upheld. No more script offers ever came Audree's way.[16]

When educators of deaf students sought to improve their drama programs, NTD initiated its Special Program for High School Teachers (1970–78) and Theatre Arts in Deaf Education (TAIDE), both popular programs in the early seventies, before lack of funds curtailed them. These programs helped educators of the deaf improve the quality of their drama programs at the day or state schools, teaching them how to direct and produce plays.

Because no deaf theater could do wholly without scripts by deaf playwrights, and in an effort to fulfill its 1966 promise to encourage deaf writers, NTD started the Deaf Playwrights Conference (DPC) in 1977.

Prior to that time, there were only three known deaf play-wrights in the United States: Howard Terry, Douglas Burke, and Eric Malzkuhn. Malzkuhn, one of the first modern deaf playwrights, like many deaf leaders, had always wanted to see more deaf playwrights.[17] In 1975, another supporter of deaf writers, Bill Moody, wrote an article for the *Deaf American* entitled "What We Need Is More Local Theatre for the Deaf!"[18] Moody, an outspoken advocate for deaf drama, saw an urgent need to seek out and train more deaf writers to become playwrights. The NTD had been aware of this need as early as 1966, and in 1977 was successful in acquiring a Ford Foundation grant to start the first annual Deaf Playwrights Conference. The DPC was patterned after the O'Neill Center's National Playwrights Conference, whose artistic director, Lloyd Richards, served as a consultant and critic for the budding deaf playwrights of DPC. (See Appendix C for a list of DPC participants.)

Between 1977 and 1982, NTD invited seventeen deaf American writers to develop new plays. Each playwright worked with a dramaturge (an expert in dramatic composition), director, stage manager, and cast, and was given two staged readings—one for the professional theatre school participants and another for the general public. Experimentation was encouraged as the playwright worked under the dramaturge's guidance. At the staged readings, seasoned hearing or deaf theater people and critics offered comments to the playwrights. At times, the audiences were asked to share their thoughts about the new works.

Of the eighteen scenes and plays presented at DPC, only two were written in the style of deaf drama. Of the seventeen DPC participants, only five have since written regularly for the stage, television, or film.

NTD awarded scholarships to past DPC participants, including Steve Baldwin, Lynn Jacobowitz, and Shanny Mow in 1979.[19] Unfortunately, DPC was put into abeyance in 1982 when the grants expired. A few much less intensive workshops have been held since 1982, but NTD is hoping to revive the original DPC format in 1994.[20]

The significance of the DPC at NTD cannot be underestimated. More than eighty plays have been produced by playwrights who attended DPC or were members of the company. The number of plays by known non-NTD people or non-DPC products is comparatively small. Appendix D lists the names of the playwrights as well as their produced works.

To meet the developmental needs of its performers, NTD, in collaboration with Connecticut College, is accredited, allowing members to earn up to six undergraduate credits. If they are graduate students, they can accumulate credit for summer school. The Master's in Fine Arts program at Connecticut College was approved in 1972.

This program allowed NTD company and staff members to take courses that lead to a master's degree in fine arts. Several members have obtained the master's in fine arts, including Dorothy Miles, Mary Beth Miller, Fanny Yeh, and Ed Waterstreet. Miles's thesis, "A History of Theatre Activities in the Deaf Community of the United States" (May 1974), has proven to be an important source of information about deaf theater.

Theatre in Sign (TIS), a small company of NTD players who perform for members of the deaf community, was started in 1979 so that NTD could better serve the deaf community. The first TIS performance included some of NTD's true stars: Phyllis Frelich and Patrick Graybill, directed by Linda Bove, acted D. L. Coburn's play about two senior citizens, *The Gin Game*. The play was presented entirely in American Sign Language without any voice actors, much to the delight of deaf playgoers, who appreciated the more natural rhythm of signs. This production was revived in the spring of 1991 with the same cast and director, this time under the auspices of Deaf West Theatre Company, a newly founded theater group in Los Angeles.

In 1980, a trio of one-act plays were produced by TIS—
Here We Are, The Bear, and *Bedtime Story.*[21] Though TIS was
popular with its audiences, the program ended in 1980, due
to lack of funding.

Storytelling, lectures, workshops, and demonstrations have
been offered by NTD at its home base between tour seasons,
during summer months, and on special holidays or weekends
since 1967. The company also helps with a summer theater institute at the Model Secondary School for the Deaf in Washington,
D.C. These programs are mostly community- and publicity-
related and have established good rapport, not only in Waterford and Chester, but also with Connecticut, New York, and
other states as well.

Few professional acting companies operate so many auxiliary
programs. And although only half of the ten NTD programs are
still active, even those that have been suspended because of
budget constraints achieved results with deaf playwrights, educators of the deaf, and the theater in general. Generally known
as a touring company, NTD has proven to be a versatile and
productive catalyst, launching and enhancing many careers in a
variety of creative, innovative, and professional ways.

NOTES

1. Andrew Vasnick, interview with author, June/July 1986.

2. John V. Van Cleve, ed., *Gallaudet Encyclopedia of Deaf People
and Deafness,* s.v. "National Theaters of the Deaf," by Shanny Mow
(New York: McGraw-Hill, 1987), 232.

3. Vasnick interview.

4. Vasnick interview.

5. Camille Jeter, interview with author, March 11, 1988.

6. "Silent Network Announces New Season Schedule," *Silent
News* (August 1988): 29.

7. Ibid.

8. Mark Hoski, NTD Spotlight, 1979–80, 2.

9. LTD Packet, 1987–88, 6.

10. *NTD Spotlight,* 1975, 8.

11. Roddy O'Connor, interview with author, July 7, 1986.

12. *LTD Playbill,* March 10, 1988.

13. Helen Powers, *Signs of Silence* (New York: Dodd, Mead, and Company, 1972), 130.

14. *NTD Olympic Issue* (1984): 6.

15. *NTD Newsletter* (Summer 1980): 1.

16. Barry Strassler, "An Applause for Audree," *Hearing Health* (June/July 1992): 14.

17. Eric Malzkuhn, "Trial and Terrors of 'Moments Preserved,'" *The Deaf American* (December 1966): 25.

18. Bill Moody, "What We Need Is More Local Theatre for the Deaf!," *The Deaf American* (September 1975): 5–6.

19. Shanny Mow, interview with author, July 8, 1986.

20. Mow interview with author, August 4, 1993.

21. *Gallaudet Encyclopedia of Deaf People and Deafness*, s. v. "National Theaters of the Deaf," by Shanny Mow, 234.

The
National
Theatre
of the
Deaf

mg

NORDDEUTSCHE KONZERTDIREKTION
MELSINE GREVESMÜHL
Triftstraße 11 · 2850 Bremerhaven 31 · Postfach 31 02 65 · Telefon (04 71) 2 8 80 68 · Telex 236 594 ball-d

CHAPTER 6
The NTD Management Team

*A*s with any organization, NTD's management sets the pace for its own success or failure. For the first few years, as the company was building its reputation as well as a growing staff, NTD was dependent upon the O'Neill Center for its general office support. Today, the management of NTD includes a tour director, general manager, costume designer, publicity director, stage manager, wardrobe supervisor, and other specialized roles, such as company interpreter and professional theater school director.

When NTD made its move to Chester, Connecticut, in 1982, the staff expanded to include additional assistants and a bookkeeper. NTD also formed its own boards: one for policy-making and one for artistic advice. The company also had to accept greater responsibility for seeking, receiving, and managing its own funds.

The Hazel E. Stark Center, located at 5 West Main Street in Chester, is composed of two buildings. To accommodate the company's growing needs, the top floor of the house has been divided into approximately ten rooms. The bottom floor is one big studio with an artist's corner, utility and storage areas, and a carpenter's shop as well. The other building, less than a hundred feet away, is actually a former mill and sits adjacent to the Pattaconk River. The mill has two levels and houses the rehearsal hall, kitchen, and a few other small rooms and storage areas. Adorning the walls are posters advertising the company's national and international tours. Countless plaques, awards, and trophies marking NTD's numerous artistic, educational, and cultural achievements grace the rooms as well.

On a normal working day, ten full-time employees, two men and eight women, work industriously—making and receiving a steady flow of phone calls. At least seven TDD calls come in daily. (A TDD is an electronic device that allows deaf people to use the telephone.) And as deaf staff members continue to be added, incoming TDD calls continue to increase.

Prior to 1981, NTD's two primary sources of income were the Department of Education grants and performing fees. Most of this money went toward traveling, touring, and overhead fees paid to the O'Neill Center for office space, meals, maintenance, and security. In addition to the Department of Education grant, the NTD has also received grants from the National Endowment for the Arts and the Connecticut Commission on the Arts. After moving to the Hazel E. Stark Center in Chester, NTD received major donations from the Eleanor Naylor Dana Charitable Trust and the Henry Luce Foundation, Inc.

After 1982, NTD began receiving corporate donations, ranging from $5,000 to $19,999, from some of America's leading corporations—IBM, Xerox, American Express, and Exxon. In 1991, the Mary Martin Memorial Fund was established in the actress's memory. This fund has reached $50,000. Grants and donations, coupled with the earnings from performances and workshops, bring the overall annual budget to about a million dollars annually. NTD now plans to set up a $500,000 endowment fund.

Some of the Far Eastern tours receive special financial support from federal funding, the ministries of foreign nations,

American embassies, media programs, cultural centers, boards of education, music societies, actors' associations, and national deaf organizations. European tours, on the other hand, have been arranged by private agencies and financed by performing fees with some help from federal funding.

Prior to the move to Chester, David Hays and David Reylea, the general manager, wrote most of the grant proposals. After the move, two full-time development staff people were added, as well as a publicity director.

Traveling around the country and the world is costly, and for these expenses, NTD has depended a great deal on its booking and performance fees to supplement foundation and government grants. As of 1993, NTD's fee for a single performance was $9,000. Additional programs, such as a performance by LTD, command $750; workshop fees vary.

Performers in the company have equal salaries with an annual cost-of-living increase and a small bonus for seniority. Regional-theater scale and longevity determine salaries, which are based on Actors' Equity scale.

The tour director books the company two years in advance. Mack Scism, the company's first tour director, served for twelve years, until his death in 1986. Booking tours on the basis of regions, NTD rotates tours to the East, Midwest, West, Southwest, and Southeast of the United States every two or three years. Some states, such as Wyoming, are visited only every three years or so, while NTD performs in New York annually. Although a few deaf organizations can afford to sponsor an NTD performance independently, the tour director always makes sure that the main sponsor has a list of local deaf organizations and individuals who can be involved. Scism developed the touring and booking system, and used his connections with regional and university theaters to build contacts over the years. A well-rounded theater professional who also directed several NTD productions and assisted Hays with the selection of voice actors, scripts, and plays, Scism contributed significantly to the growth of NTD. After Scism's death, Roddy O'Connor became NTD's second tour director, a post he still holds at this writing.

Since NTD must function in a hearing world, interpreters are also important members of the staff. As company interpreter from 1967 to 1982, then again from 1986 to the present, Nikki Kilpatrick is a hearing, certified American Sign Language interpreter whose parents are deaf. Since most of the guest directors, playwrights, lecturers, and visitors are nonsigners, there is an ongoing need for the interpreter's services. In addition to her interpreting role, Kilpatrick has long sponsored the summer-school fencing finals, and the winner's name is engraved on a trophy named after Kilpatrick's parents.

A considerable number of people on the staff, including the production stage manager and other hearing program directors, or even voice actors, have filled in as interpreters during touring seasons. During the summer, three professional interpreters volunteer their services in return for room and board.

The NTD also employs a general manager. From 1977 to 1990, David Relyea, experienced in the management of Broadway and off-Broadway productions, oversaw the finances of the company. When he left in 1990, Ed Coffield, a former performing production stage manager, was hired to replace him.

A founding member of NTD, Andrew Vasnick began serving as NTD's director of the Professional School for Deaf Theatre Personnel in 1979. Vasnick is also the only deaf person to have served on the NTD board of directors. Vasnick's wife, Sandi Inches, was also a longtime member of the company. Both Vasnick and Inches left NTD in 1991.

Many other staff members have contributed significantly toward the growth of NTD. Patrick Graybill has served as summer-school director, actor, and also as a guest lecturer; Shanny Mow contributed his talents as DPC director, actor, and playwright; Betty Beekman, who has deaf parents, served as a production stage manager and company manager; Laine Dyer has filled the role of publicity director for a number of years;

Leonora Hays, David's wife, has assisted as a development consultant and NTD representative at many functions; and Beth House has been active as the advocacy director. In addition to these paid staff members, many volunteers have worked in NTD's Chester office.

In the spring of 1991, NTD announced that Julianna Fjeld had been appointed co-artistic director. As previously mentioned, Fjeld had already carved a niche in the entertainment field with an Emmy for her work as co-executive producer of the popular made-for-television drama "Love Is Never Silent." After working five years as an actress for NTD, from 1971 to 1975, Fjeld moved to Los Angeles, where she appeared in films and television. She also helped create Deaf Audience Theatre Experience (D.A.T.E.) and worked as a consultant and actress for the Tony Award–winning play *Children of a Lesser God.*

However, less than two years later, in December 1992, Fjeld unexpectedly resigned. According to the March 1993 issue of the *Silent News,* the "circumstances surrounding her departure (in late December) remained unclear."[1] Additionally, Fjeld cited a contract clause in her letter of resignation that prevented her from making any public or private comments to the press. Rumors have circulated that the reason for the resignation was artistic disagreements between Fjeld and Hays over play selection. Apparently, Fjeld had wanted to do a revival of *My Third Eye,* while Hays saw no commercial or artistic merit in the idea.

Camille Jeter, a third-generation deaf person and a member of NTD since 1986, became the new artistic director early in 1993. Then in May 1993, NTD announced that Will Rhys, a founding member and guest director, had been appointed as the second artistic director of the company. Jeter and Rhys have assumed the operational and artistic responsibilities of NTD, while David Hays, the founding artistic director, is now concentrating his efforts on raising funds for NTD.

One other NTD member has become part of the management team. Nat Wilson is the coordinator of the NTD outreach program. He began this job in the fall of 1992 and is responsible for managing a three-year grant of $450,000. The goal of the outreach program is to increase the number of deaf playgoers from 10 to 15 percent.[2]

To accomplish this, an advance team is sent to places where NTD will perform so that the deaf community will know more about the upcoming production. The team also teaches the sponsors how to publicize NTD appearances by contacting the various segments within the deaf community and other programs related to deafness.

The addition of these two deaf administrators has begun to change the company. Prior to Fjeld's arrival, David Hays had taken sole responsibility for administering the touring company and main office on a daily basis. Since NTD tours eight months annually, the artistic director sees that the sets, costumes, lights, and stage properties can withstand the constant traveling. Furthermore, two-way communication for the predominantly deaf performers must be ensured. Hays and Jeter are flooded with requests for interviews, which include the inevitable questions about NTD's performance style, as well as questions about deafness, sign language, and the deaf population. Like the rest of the staff, Hays and Jeter also fill other roles: photographer, scene and light designer, director, and playwright.

With the addition of a second artistic director, what will the future hold for David Hays? Often described as "a man of few words," Hays told this writer on March 20, 1992, that he hopes to have fewer administrative responsibilities and that he plans to focus on raising capital for NTD in the years to come.

When Hays decided to start a theater of the deaf, he demonstrated two valuable traits: perseverance and fortitude. Hays thrived on the challenge of working with amateur deaf actors and actresses, and he was eventually able to make NTD a "breeding ground for the most professional performers."[3] Hays and NTD have provided acting training for more than 580 deaf and hearing people over a span of twenty-five years. (These figures combine the total of company members and summer-school participants.) He endured early "barnstorming days" and presented a performing minority group to a skeptical public across the country and overseas, both daring and risky projects to begin with. Like the adventurous sailor he is, Hays yearned for greater seas for the company. Hays had all the contacts, sources, and initial backing needed. He also used his friendships with many Broadway professionals to interest them in working with NTD. With his academic background and professional expertise, he put his talents to use for the artistic development of NTD. As the founding father, his work with NTD has been nothing less than a labor of love.

While it is important to note the work of the NTD staff, it is equally important to look at the company's influence as indicated by its alumni's continued work in theater, film, and television. Perhaps the most famous production involving NTD actors was *Children of a Lesser God*. Phyllis Frelich, a founding member of NTD, and her husband, Robert Steinberg, an NTD stage manager in 1967, met Mark Medoff in 1978. The three worked together to develop a play about a deaf woman's life, loosely based on Frelich and Steinberg's marriage. The play had its early development at New Mexico State University, where Medoff was drama department chairperson, and was later performed at the Mark Taper Forum in Los Angeles, under the direction of Gordon Davidson. There, Julianna Fjeld was hired as one of the consultants for the play.[4] *Children of a Lesser God* then moved to the Longacre Theatre in New York, where it won three Tony awards in 1980. Besides winning the award for best play, it also garnered best actress and best actor awards for Frelich and John Rubinstein. This Broadway production also employed Robert Steinberg as understudy to Rubinstein. Richard Kendall and Linda Bove, two more NTD alumni, were also understudies in New York and later were in the road company for *Children*. The play ran for 887 performances in New York, finally closing in 1982.[5]

After working with the Mark Taper Forum, Julianna Fjeld served as co-executive producer of NBC's Hallmark television movie "Love Is Never Silent" (1985), which won the Emmy for best drama in 1986. Several NTD alumni took part in this movie; Frelich and Ed Waterstreet played the leading roles, while Fjeld and Lou Fant played minor roles.

In addition to work in plays and movies, NTD performers have appeared in numerous television productions, including soap operas, children's shows, and prime-time programs such as "Mannix" (Audree Norton), "Happy Days" (Linda Bove), "Barney Miller" and "Spenser for Hire" (Phyllis Frelich), "Cagney and Lacy" (Peter Wolf), and "The Equalizer" and "Hunter" (Howie Seago). Several local and regional theaters also have employed NTD actors and actresses in hearing plays that were slightly modified to accommodate a deaf performer. Bernard Bragg, Howie Seago, Andy Vasnick, Mike Lamitola, Julianna Fjeld, Lewis Merkin, Jean St. Clair, and several other NTD alumni performed in hearing productions that were neither deaf theater nor sign-language theater. The influence of NTD on these plays, movies, and television series is clear, since so many of the performers and advisers have come from NTD.

On March 18, 1989, the Oklahoma School for the Deaf (OSD) became the first theater to revive an NTD production, *Gianni Schicchi* (1967). With permission from NTD, former superintendent and NTD founding member Ralph White arranged to have the play produced. Bernard Bragg, also an NTD founding member, directed the nonoperatic version of Puccini's opera. The OSD students won the "Best of Show" award at the Third Annual Very Special Arts Festival for Deaf Students (also founded by White) held at the Louisiana School for the Deaf in Baton Rouge.

Although NTD is essentially a theater of the deaf, the company has played a significant role in establishing theaters both of and for the deaf. Before 1970, there were deaf theater or literary groups in major cities (San Francisco, Chicago, Washington, D.C., New York, Los Angeles, and Philadelphia) that performed sporadically. Then, in the seventies, new theaters began to spring up elsewhere. In 1973, the Experimental Theatre Department was established by Robert Panara at the National Institute for the Deaf in Rochester, New York. This theater was later renamed "The Robert F. Panara Theatre" in 1988.[6]

More than twenty other deaf theater groups followed, many of which were not able to continue operations. While some of the groups are still in existence, most have struggled to stay afloat, such as Fairmount Theatre of the Deaf (Ohio). There is one group, however, Deaf West Theatre Company (1991), in Los Angeles, that has created a great deal of excitement in the deaf community. Founded by former NTD members, this young company has been awarded a three-year grant to take them through 1995.

Largely due to the perseverance and dedication of its longtime staff, NTD has achieved and continues its success as a national and international touring troupe. Entering its twenty-sixth consecutive year (1992–93), NTD and many of its former members can claim an impressive list of professional achievements in theater, film, and television.

NOTES

1. "Julianna Fjeld Leaves Position with National Theatre of the Deaf," *Silent News* (March 1993):1.

2. Nat Wilson, interview with author, March 21, 1992.

3. Alan P. Sanoff, 'The Power of Unspoken Words," *U.S. News and World Report,* November 10, 1986, 83.

4. Steve Baldwin, "Julianna Fjeld: More Than Just A Dream," *The Deaf Texan* (May 1987): 10.

5. Otis L. Guernesey, Jr., ed., *The Best Plays of 1981–1982* (New York: Dodd, Mead and Company, 1983), 308.

6. "NTID's Theatre Named After Robert F. Panara," *Silent News* (July 1988): 1.

CHAPTER 7

Creating Pictures in the Air

*N*TD's most distinguishing feature—its performance style—has won and sustained interest for more than twenty-five years. Its primary component, sign language, sets NTD apart from other professional theaters.

To the majority of the performers (that is, the deaf performers), sign language, and not necessarily English, is the primary language. American Sign Language (ASL) syntax is different from English syntax, and most of its signs are arbitrary. For example, some universal signs, such as EAT, SLEEP, SMALL, and LOVE, are naturally gestured. Other signs are expressed symbolically and abstractly. The emotional quality of a particular sign such as ANGRY can be controlled by the intensity of the movement and appropriate facial expressions. American Sign Language, as a manual or visual/gestural language, replaces spoken language, thus allowing signers to use their hands to express their poetic imaginations.

Two linguists, Edward A. Klima and Ursula Bellugi, have written exclusively on the language of the deaf.

Many years ago, when we first began to study ASL, we read that sign language was "a collection of vague and loosely defined pictorial gestures"; that it was characterized by "grammatical disorder, illogical systems, and linguistic confusion"; and it was a pidgin form of English in the hands with no structure of its own." Although these views have been dispelled, most people are not aware of the poetic tradition developing in the language. This tradition shows how human beings, deprived of spoken language, devise ways to express the poetic imagination.[1]

In gathering evidence for their article "Poetry Without Sound," Klima and Bellugi used members of NTD, among them Bernard Bragg, Dorothy Miles, Lou Fant, and Shanny Mow, to demonstrate how poems could be signed. Klima and Bellugi were especially interested in the poems of e.e. cummings, and as a result of their study, they concluded that poetry signers are innately poetical, spatial, kinetic, temporal, and rhythmic, depending on the variations in the signs and the preferred style of the signer.

The study by Klima and Bellugi also suggests why, upon first seeing *Our Town* at Gallaudet in 1961, David Hays coined the phrase "sculpture in the air." Consequently, NTD frequently has used the slogan, "You see every word you hear." Because of its very nature, signing's flexibility and visual aspect are analogous to using the hands as a chisel and taking an imaginary block of marble, from which one can create different images.[2]

Hays and others recognized that within ASL usage there was much variation and movement, orientation, and intensity. These qualities were especially evident when Audree Norton signed Elizabeth Browning's forty-third sonnet, "How Do I Love Thee? Let Me Count the Ways," for NTD in 1968.

Shanny Mow once said that NTD signers make economic, creative, artistic, clever, and theatrical interpretation of the script without sacrificing the spirit of the writer's language. Like stage voices, signs must be larger-than-life and expressed theatrically, depending on the type of play performed.[3]

Over the last twenty-five years, Hays has made countless statements to the media, some of which may provide clues as to how he came to visualize a theater of the deaf as a major art form. In the spring of 1985, he defined his visually rich theater based on signing as

A unique form that combines spoken theatre, dance, signing, and pantomime. To me, there is something inexpressive, stilted, and almost boring about the actor opening and closing a little hole in the lower middle of his face. Wonderful, meaningful noise emerges, but if only he could do that with his arms, his knees, his shoulders, his fingers—and have his full face not just "in support" but as something read. And with signing, every part of the body works to inflect color, to tilt the word towards full emotional meaning—the speed, the placement, the facial expression.[4]

To Hays, deaf people "are the very best at doing the specific kind of theatre they do."[5] He believes in the semiotic aspects of theater, combining both sight and sound to produce sculptures in the air.[6] Hays states:

Watch the language in the air and you will find a suddenly sharper, clearer understanding of the spoken word. It's akin to the phenomenon of your memory of a captioned foreign film.[7]

Here again, Hays is thinking of the power of signification, "where you see and hear every word," another frequently used NTD phrase.

Most deaf people spend their whole lives communicating externally. When making an effort to communicate with nonsigning, oral/aural persons, deaf people necessarily translate everything into acting through simple and clear facial expressions or simplified body language. To a certain degree, deaf people, out of communicative necessity, become actors. Deaf people are not necessarily gifted actors, per se, but acting comes more naturally to them than to hearing people. The need to articulate nonverbally requires disciplined concentration. Through sign language, the spoken lines are visually illuminated by NTD's deaf performers. The "quiet" communication is then reinforced by the voices of the professional hearing onstage actors and actresses, and appropriate on- or offstage sounds or music. Hays first noticed this synthesis of elements when he saw a performance at Gallaudet in 1961.[8] For Hays, the visual and physical aspect of NTD acting creates an aesthetic synthesis. In this way, sign language is transformed into an art form on the stage. Hays's stated artistic goal for NTD became "to present a visual language . . . that would be theatricalized and made central."[9]

Sound and music are also an important part of NTD productions. In the earlier NTD days, onstage vibrating, sculptured musical instruments, designed by François and Bernard Baschet, were used. The deaf cast could sometimes feel the vibrations from these instruments and use them as cues. The instruments were also used as mood-setting devices. *The Iliad* (1980) used drums in its half-time activities, and *All the Way Home* (1984) made use of an organ; these conventional instruments emit lower-frequency sounds, which most profoundly deaf people can hear or feel.

When the company develops scripts reflecting deaf themes, deafness may be indicated only symbolically. For example, in *The Wooden Boy: The Secret Life of Geppetto's Dummy* (1979) by David Hays, written after Collodi's *Pinocchio,* Pinocchio's woodenness is partially used to symbolize deafness. In other plays, deafness is treated overtly, such as in Mow and Hays's *Parzival, From the Horse's Mouth* (1982), where the actors step out of themselves and talk about their own search as deaf persons for the Holy Grail. In *All the Way Home* (1984), the family is deaf, instead of hearing, as in Tad Mosel's original play. The hearing boy in the play functions as an interpreter and is the only hearing person in the family, except for the voice actors, who play nonfamily hearing roles.

Shanny Mow became the first and only deaf playwright to have four of his works produced by NTD. PHOTO BY A. VINCENT SCARANO, COURTESY OF NTD

Mow's *The Iliad, Play by Play* was a Homeric spoof of the Super Bowl (*left to right*: Nat Wilson, Adrian Blue, and Howie Seago). PHOTO COURTESY OF NTD

Mow's second comedy, *The Ghost of Chastity Past*, starred Akihiro Yonaiyama of Japan (*left to right*: Andy Vasnick, Michael Lamitola, and Akihiro Yonaiyama). PHOTO COURTESY OF NTD

In 1984, NTD was one of the four American companies invited to perform at the Olympic Arts Festival in Los Angeles. In this scene from *The Hero with a Thousand Faces*, the cast depicts a sailing ship. PHOTO COURTESY OF NTD

The Little Theatre of the Deaf presented *A Child's Christmas in Wales* in 1987. This production is a traditional NTD holiday stage and television presentation (*left to right*: Cathleen Riddley, John Eisner, Willy Conley, Michael Lamitola, and Sandi Inches). PHOTO BY A. VINCENT SCARANO, COURTESY OF NTD

Artist-actor Chuck Baird paints Willy Conley's crown in *King of Hearts*. This is the only NTD production based on a film. PHOTO BY J RANELLI, COURTESY OF NTD

The staff and students of the Professional Theatre School at Chester, Connecticut (1986). The building is a former mill, one of two buildings donated by Irving Stark to NTD as a memorial to his wife, Hazel. PHOTO COURTESY OF NTD

The ensemble cast of The Little Theatre of the Deaf often performs for young audiences in public schools. Here the cast creates a star at the request of the audience. LTD has a larger booking schedule than its parent company. PHOTO COURTESY OF NTD

Another talented and entertaining LTD ensemble performed at Emerson's Majestic Theatre in Boston, Massachusetts. PHOTO BY A. VINCENT SCARANO, COURTESY OF NTD

The advanced group of the 1986 NTD Professional School for Deaf Theatre Personnel presents an improvised story on Chester Village Green before a Sunday afternoon crowd. PHOTOS BY AUTHOR

A rest stop in the Allegheny foothills for Nat Wilson, Sandi Vasnick, Andy Vasnick, and Adrian Blue. Tedious bus trips and one-night stands have become a way of life for the NTD troupe over the past twenty-five years. PHOTO BY WILLY CONLEY

Keeping in touch with the NTD home office and the next host sponsor is the primary responsibility of the production stage manager (Fred Noel). PHOTO BY WILLY CONLEY

Julianna Fjeld, a deaf actor and producer, became the first co-artistic director of NTD. Her brief sojourn lasted from 1991 to 1992. PHOTO BY YORK, COURTESY OF NTD

Camille Jeter became the associate artistic director in 1993. Recipient of the Princess Grace Foundation–USA Theatre Fellowship in 1990, Jeter has worked for NTD since 1986. She became artistic director, along with Will Rhys, in late 1993. PHOTO COURTESY OF NTD

In 1993, David Hays, founding artistic director of NTD, began to concentrate his efforts on fund-raising. PHOTO COURTESY OF NTD

The 1990–1991 company posed for this group photo (*bottom left to right:* Robert DeMayo, Camille L. Jeter, Tommy Cheng; *middle left to right:* David Hays, Kymberli Colbourne, Josif Schneiderman; *top left to right:* Susan Jackson, Adrian Blue, Chuck Baird, Mark Allen Branson, Nat Wilson). PHOTO COURTESY OF NTD

Our Town by Thornton Wilder was produced by NTD in 1979. This production was a classic example of how NTD adapts established plays into its performance style. (PHOTO COURTESY OF NTD)

Songs from Milk Wood was an important production during the 1969–1970 tour season. Dorothy S. Miles (*center*), a founding member of the company, called the production a turning point in NTD's history. NTD's 1993–1994 season included a revival entitled *Under Milk Wood* dedicated to the memory of Dot Miles. PHOTO COURTESY OF NTD

A considerable number of Dylan Thomas's works have been produced by NTD over the years. The production of *Quite Early One Morning* contributed to the success of the 1978–1979 tour season. TOP PHOTO BY ROBERT STEINBERG, COURTESY OF NTD; BOTTOM PHOTO COURTESY OF NTD

During NTD's foreign tours, productions sometimes become trilingual, as in the Chinese tour of *Farewell, My Lovely,* where Lily Han could be seen on the far left side speaking Mandarin while the company's voice actress was speaking English, both interpreting for the deaf performers. Thus, three languages— signs, English, and Mandarin—were being used simultaneously.

The company's performance style can be further defined by looking at some of its most successful productions. Four representative productions have been selected for brief examination: *Songs from Milk Wood, Quite Early One Morning, Volpone,* and *Our Town.*

Songs from Milk Wood (1969) established that sound is not the only means of expressing Dylan Thomas's poetry. According to Shanny Mow, *Songs from Milk Wood* was the production that first brought NTD's performance style into focus.

> People realized that an actor can use his hands to express the imagery aspect of the Thomas work, either singly or collectively . . . slow or quick . . . and do it better than voice. It became fascinating to watch something that is done with the hands. For example, the case [for *Milk Wood*] all share one line together, singly, alternatively, trio, duet, and group, and the voice can start and finish the line at the same time. Another example from the production is how a sailboat is caught in a storm in a very visual and graphic way. [Translated from ASL.][10]

This production was among the first to demonstrate fully the aesthetic style of NTD. As noted by Dorothy Miles, who adapted the play with Bernard Bragg, *Milk Wood* earned the respect of both critics and playgoers.[11]

A second representative production is *Quite Early One Morning* (1978), another poem by Dylan Thomas. The poem contains many visual images and graphic motifs, and the narrative nature of the poem made it suitable for NTD's way of using narrators.

The company made optimal use of its performance style by showing once again how sign language as an art form for the stage can be used to create great variety. With its innovative presentation, the cast actually heightened the poetic quality of the poem.

Volpone (1978) was performed on the same bill as *Quite Early One Morning*. Based on an adaptation by Stefan Zweig of Ben Jonson's play, quick action and signing, colorful costumes, and adaptable sets all contributed to the success of this play. Wide vocal ranges from the hearing actors were required, as well as the synchronization of their performance with the signing. These two productions proved to be one of NTD's most successful double bills.

These three plays appealed mostly to the hearing, nonsigning members of the audience. With the probable exception of *Volpone,* part of the deaf audience would not rate the other two productions as highly as it would *My Third Eye* (1971) and *Parade* (1975), which were the closest to deaf theater that NTD has ever come.

The fourth representative production, Thornton Wilder's *Our Town,* offers the opportunity to visualize most freely how NTD prepares a play to fit the components of its performing style. Fortunately, the production was videotaped in 1979, and an actor's annotated script is available. Together, they provide evidence of how NTD adapts and performs established plays. This production was specially funded by the government of Japan, where it was first presented in the summer of 1979.

Directed by Mack Scism, David Hays designed the set and lights; costumes were designed by Fred Voelpel. The carefully annotated script belongs to Shanny Mow, who played Morgan in the drugstore scene, a newspaperboy, and a member of the church choir.

According to Mow's notes, even after more than twenty-three pages of lines were cut, the playing time was still two hours and twenty-three minutes. At least three characters out of seventeen were omitted to accommodate the standard NTD troupe of eleven deaf performers and three voice performers (two males and one female). Other cuts involved offstage and certain onstage sounds—trains, animals, and weather sounds; dialogue of actors with the audience, which can be very inconvenient for deaf playgoers; several characters—the Professor, Howie, Frankie, and other "extras" such as the ballplayers; difficult-to-translate hearing idioms ("bite the word"); references that would be made only in a hearing society ("I haven't heard a sound out of her"); local American places ("Clinton, New York"); and human whistling sounds.

The script also shows how some "sound" words or lines were modified to suit the nature of the deaf cast. For example, Dr. Gibbs said he "saw" instead of "heard your mother chopping wood." When Emily and George agreed to communicate from each other's house at night, they "waved" instead of "whistled" when sharing their school assignments. Even some hearing idioms were translated into ASL. For example, "lots of hens gossiping on the corner" became "group women gossip down corner." The three voice performers played a prominent role in the production, demonstrating a remarkable range of voice characterizations. Treated as a natural part of the whole staging, the voice actors also "cued" the deaf performers by entering, exiting, standing, or just moving ahead.

In his script, Mow made notes on particular signs or handshapes for certain lines. He used a one-handed GOOD MORNING," instead of the standard two-handed greeting, to make the sign appear more casual in dialogue.

The set by David Hays was sparse: benches, ladders, a tree, lamp, chairs, and a small platform. Such a set, as suggested by Thornton Wilder, is easy to move, pack, assemble, and use in different theaters, and is easily transported by truck or plane.

Scenery is given a simple, light, versatile, and portable design for most productions. The demand for ensemble mobility greatly influences the design of sets and costumes. Both are kept simple and safe for the quickly moving performers. Lighting designers, too, must always be aware of the rapid stage movements.

Designers are governed by such principles that befit a touring company that practically lives out of a suitcase, performing mostly one-night stands.

Lighting on stage right in Act Three when the "dead" townspeople conversed with the recently deceased Emily allowed for an emotional but restrained scene. The lights played on the emotionless faces and stiff signing hands of the deaf performers who were seated facing the audience. (Three voice actors were also in the cemetery, but they were turned sideways so they could see the signing performers.) Wilder had insisted that performers in this play "maintain a continual dryness of tone"; this was achieved by use of the lights, suggesting the "dryness" of the signs in combination with the facial expressions of the deaf cast.

Fred Voelpel's costumes appropriately fit the period for the play and were not too flashy or loose-fitting. The light, thin materials allowed for considerable physical action on the stage, and the hands and faces were not obscured by any clothing that would have interfered with signing.

Certain principles sometimes govern the designs for lighting, sets, and costumes. Due to the fact that NTD tours widely, mostly by bus and truck, the sets and costumes are designed to fit the size of a truck. As for the lights, only special lighting equipment is brought along. The road stage manager and his crew set the lights wherever they perform. However, the company manager obtains stage dimensions and lights prior to the performance and passes the information along to the crew during touring. In the case of *Our Town,* the cast rehearsed in the Rose Barn Theater at the O'Neill Theatre Center, where they experimented with a typical stage size.

Each of the fourteen characters in *Our Town* has a particular name sign. For example, George's name sign is introduced early by the stage manager, who first fingerspells the name slowly and clearly, then moves the fingerspelled letter *G* to his right temple. Once all the name signs are established, the deaf audience is able to follow the play easily.

The wedding scene was particularly interesting. A raised platform upstage center became the focal point, while the aisle created perspective, diminishing from the first downstage row toward the platform, where the minister stood elevated above the stage so his signing could be seen clearly.

Just as the deaf playgoer perceived NTD productions differently from the nonsigning hearing audience, the deaf critic does not always agree with the hearing critic. The hearing critic depends a good deal on the voice actors; the deaf critic is often unable to adequately interpret the signing because of poor lighting, distracting stage movements, and "hearing" themes. So it is not surprising that a "deaf" review and a "hearing" review reveal interesting cultural differences and needs.

About 90 percent of the NTD audience is comprised of nonsigning hearing people, and it has been nonsigning hearing theater critics who have done the most to foster public acceptance of NTD as an integral part of the American stage. Following are some representative critical comments by hearing critics about the company's performance style:

NTD is not just handicapped people making the best of things. It is true theatre ... powerful, funny, touching ... standing on its own art form.[12]

Graceful visual imagery of sign language is used to enhance the spoken word.[13]

A distinctive and highly visual performing style.[14]

... creating something beautiful to the eye as well as communicating the thoughts and words of the play.[15]

With ingenious pantomime, the performers showed the children how to act out a simple fairy tale or folk story, their actions far superseding the sign language of the deaf.[16]

Language of the hands seems to be a beautiful art form itself.[17]

[Sign language] achieves a beauty and sweep that makes it particularly effective on stage.[18]

Not all hearing critics or observers agreed:

[NTD should use] graphic symbols indicating, often with great expressiveness, things such as a river or snowstorm. Then these talented actors would have a far better opportunity to act rather than merely gesticulate, however beautifully and sensitively such gesticulations are made.[19]

It is beautiful to watch the [NTD] actors create. They start with very little—a favorite little song, some second-hand information—then they make it their own. But I think deaf playwrights need to be developed. Surely they have their own way of looking at the world.[20]

The important point, however, is that the majority of critics view NTD as a theater with a highly developed aesthetic sense.

Yet not all NTD productions have been successful. Such plays as *Four Saints in Three Acts* (1976) and *All the Way Home* (1984) failed because the director or script either did not or could not utilize the NTD performing style fully or effectively. Despite the talented cast and the appropriate physical blocking, *Four Saints in Three Acts* failed to impress either the hearing or deaf audiences. Perhaps it was a poor script choice and did not appeal to the taste of most playgoers, hearing or deaf.

Credit should be given to the NTD actors who strive to make their unique performing style as entertaining as possible. At the same time, they do not compromise the intent of the writer's premise or message. As they perform a piece, the actors have proven time after time that sign language does enhance the spoken or written language as a valid art form. The audience, therefore, experiences the play from a very visual perspective, in an enlightening way.

Whether it is an established play that can best suit the unique performing style of NTD or a company-developed script, the performers combine all the essential components, visually, physically, and aesthetically, to produce sculptures and pictures in the air.

NOTES

1. Edward A. Klima and Ursula Bellugi, "Poetry Without Sound," *Human Nature* (October 1978): 83.

2. Shanny Mow, interview with author, November 18, 1988.

3. Mow interview.

4. Bob Hicks, "Theatre of Deaf Fuses Voice, Sign Language, Good Acting," (n.p., 1985).

5. Hicks.

6. Lester Brooks, "Sculptures in the Air," *Sky Magazine* (July 1986, 32–39): 34.

7. Brooks, 36.

8. David Hays, interview with author, March 10, 1988.

9. Brooks, 34.

10. Mow interview.

11. Dorothy S. Miles, "A History of Theatre Activities in the Deaf Community of the United States," Master's thesis, Connecticut College, 1974, 62.

12. Delores Hughes, "In the Theatre," n.p., October 25, 1985.

13. Andy Smith, "Words, Seen and Spoken, Produce Fine Drama for the Deaf, Hearing," *Democrat and Chronicle* (Rochester, N.Y.), October 17, 1985.

14. Smith.

15. John Griffin, "Sign Language More Than Just Words, Actor Says," *Middleton Journal* (Ohio), February 22, 1985.

16. Linda DuVal, "Children Learn Actions Speak Louder Than Words in Theatre of the Deaf," *Gazette Telegraph* (Colorado Springs), n.d., n.p.

17. Helen Powers, *Signs of Silence* (New York: Dodd, Mead and Company, 1972), 130.

18. Edwin Wilson, "The National Theatre of the Deaf," *The Wall Street Journal,* February 19, 1985.

19. George McClendon, "The Unique Contributions of the National Theatre of the Deaf to the American Theatre," Master's thesis, Catholic University, 1972, 95.

20. John Heidger, "The Theatre of the Deaf in America: The Silent Stage," Master's thesis, Southern Illinois University, 1979, 54.

The National Theatre of the Deaf presents

King of Hearts

They are a National Treasure. You'll Hear <u>and See</u> Every Word.

CHAPTER 8

In Retrospect, With an Eye to the Future

T he history of NTD is the record of those people and groups who nourished and helped it grow into a major acting company. Using sign language as a serious theatrical device, NTD, over a period of twenty-five years, has become a vital part of American deaf and hearing theaters.

In addition to being a first-rate professional acting company, NTD is also an intercultural company, borrowing freely from foreign works, as well as from creations of its own. Richard Schechner defines intercultural performance in this way:

> What is borrowed is swiftly transformed into native material . . . at the very same time as the borrowing re-makes native culture. So human cultures . . . the most traditional even . . . when viewed holistically, are something like the earth viewed from near-space: a whirling mass of constantly changing patterns, incorporating what is introduced, sending out feelers into the surround: very active, yet very organized.[1]

A considerable number of NTD productions derived from other cultures, but were reconstructed through sign language. The multinational presentation at the 1988 Tokyo festival was

NTD's most important intercultural project. During this international presentation, NTD joined forces with deaf actors from Japan, China, Russia, and India.

Reconstructing plays out of improvisations, themes, radio plays, novels, and films is a creative process that depends primarily on the sense of sight, rendering the text in visual terms for the audience. This approach was nothing new to the deaf community. Edna Levine had known about it before NTD was formed. Then when Anne Bancroft, Gene Lasko, Arthur Penn, and David Hays came to recognize the potential of sign language as an art form, their enthusiasm evolved into a special partnership with the deaf community. Both hearing and deaf persons played a significant role in developing the notion of a theater of the deaf.

The hearing half of the theater dichotomy included Levine, Bancroft, George White, the O'Neill Center, Mary Switzer, and a host of Broadway people. Hays once said of Switzer that she "illuminated the dark profile of the entire [deaf] population."[2] Hays's involvement has obviously been critical to the entire history—and success—of NTD.

The deaf half of the dichotomy developed out of grass-roots theaters, Gallaudet University, consultants, NAD, and governmental agencies, particularly the Vocational Rehabilitation Administration (Boyce R. Williams and Malcolm Norwood). Laws pertaining to the education of handicapped people, especially the amendments of 1986 (part F), eventually assured permanent funding for the National Theatre of the Deaf.[3]

The cultural revolution of the sixties helped to make NTD acceptable to hearing audiences. Agitation for social change, such as the civil rights movement, also helped to pave the way for NTD. Hansberry's *A Raisin in the Sun* and other ethnic plays led the way for theaters dealing with minorities and people with disabilities.

In the deaf world, many of the social and economic improvements over the past twenty-five years are often credited to NTD.

Although there has been no controlled study to measure the impact of NTD on the betterment of life for deaf people, there are credible studies and books that recognize NTD as a major force in bringing about change. The writings of Taras B. Denis are especially persuasive. Leo Jacobs's *A Deaf Adult Speaks Out* (1974) argues that NTD influenced the employment of the deaf in the performing arts and thereby improved "the image of sign language and deafness."[4] Jack R. Gannon, a nationally known deaf writer, includes a twelve-page discussion of NTD in his book *Deaf Heritage: A Narrative History of Deaf America* (1981).[5] Dr. Roslyn Rosen, noted deaf leader and president of NAD from 1990 to 1993, considers NTD to be a major "catalytic event that bewitched and educated deaf and hearing audiences."[6] Professor and author Alan B. Crammatte rates NTD as one of the major factors in expanding the work opportunities for deaf professionals in America.[7] Even during the early years of NTD, a study entitled "A Survey of Theatre Activities in American and Canadian Schools for the Deaf 1965–1970" correlated the growth of deaf-school drama programs with the emergence of NTD.[8] Another survey traced the phenomenal growth of sign-language classes and interpreter training programs at the junior- and community-college levels and gave some of the credit for this development to NTD.[9] References to NTD in studies and books have become commonplace and warrant further research. Further study is also needed to ascertain NTD's influence in foreign countries.

Earlier it was noted that from 1967 to around 1980, NTD was not always well received by the deaf community. Common complaints centered around NTD's fast signing and its overuse of the hearing-world culture and themes with slight emphasis on deaf culture. This same sentiment was expressed by Michael A. Schwartz, a lawyer, mime, and former NTD actor (1977–1978) in the April 1993 issue of *Silent News*. Schwartz wrote that NTD is not a true deaf theater, yet he failed to distinguish between theater *of* the deaf and theater *for* the deaf. He advocated that deaf theater reflect deaf culture and the experiences of the deaf community.[10]

However, as mentioned earlier, the deaf community has begun to recognize NTD as a positive social force. As the years have gone by, and as the reputation of NTD has grown stronger, more and more deaf critics have discontinued their tirades against NTD. Typical of those critics is Leo Burke of Baton Rouge, Louisiana. Burke founded the Hartford Thespians (1973–78), a well-known deaf theater that rebelled against NTD's sign-language theater style. According to Burke, he, along with many other deaf critics, eventually realized that NTD had done more social good than harm. He realized that the dislike of NTD had decreased as deaf theatergoers began to grow accustomed to NTD's style of performing. Over the years, Burke, like many deaf critics, learned to appreciate NTD's contributions.[11]

The addition of the NTD outreach department should also help to bridge the gap between NTD and the deaf community. This department offers free lectures, demonstrations, and programs wherever NTD performs.

As NTD continues to grow, it is considering several options. NTD plans to venture more aggressively into television, movies, and videos, recognizing the benefits from its own past television programs and that many of its alumni have gone on to work in these media.

Expansion would require more staffing, particularly of people who are deaf. Prior to the hiring of Julianna Fjeld, Nat Wilson, and Camille Jeter, only Andrew Vasnick, Shanny Mow, and Patrick Graybill had offered deaf representation on the administrative staff.

Another change may be needed in the repertoire of NTD. Both deaf and hearing audiences have expressed the desire to see more comedies. Since deaf people often seem to be natural comedians, comic talent needs to be developed and explored.

Still other changes involve the need to reinstate such inactive programs as Theatre in Sign and the Deaf Playwrights Conference. In the last few years, several people with close ties to NTD, including Eric Malzkuhn, Robert Panara, and Michael Schwartz, have enjoined NTD to produce the works of deaf playwrights. One way to accomplish this is to revive the Deaf Playwrights Conference. Lastly, the schedule of the Professional Theatre School and the number of NTD rehearsals need to be lengthened in order to reduce the stress created by the current heavy schedule.

One essential fact is that the NTD ensemble has no established stars. Its plays are developed from existing or original materials, and it utilizes a rich and physical language that adds a new dimension to the stage.

All in all, America's most active theater company appears to have a bright future. NTD has earned a niche in the world of theater, both at home and abroad. Since 1967, NTD has proven that sign language can be used successfully as a creative art form for the stage.

The National Theatre of the Deaf developed from a notion that sign language possesses its own power and beauty, and it has blossomed into a major acting company that continues almost thirty-four years later to "delight and instruct" people all over the world.

NOTES

1. Richard Schechner, "Intercultural Performance," *Drama Review* 26 (Summer 1982): 3.

2. David Hays, interview with author, July 10, 1986.

3. Malcolm J. Norwood, letter to author, September 25, 1988.

4. Leo Jacobs, *A Deaf Adult Speaks Out* (Washington, D.C.: Gallaudet University Press, 1974), 119.

5. Jack Gannon, *Deaf Heritage: A Narrative History of Deaf America,* (Silver Spring, Md.: National Association of the Deaf, 1981), 344–56.

6. Roslyn Rosen, "Deafness: A Social Perspective," in *Deafness in Perspective,* ed. David Luterman (San Diego: College-Hill Press, 1986), 257.

7. Alan B. Crammatte, *Meeting the Challenge: Hearing-Impaired Professionals in the Workplace,* (Washington, D.C.: Gallaudet University Press, 1987), 7, 9.

8. Jackson Davis, "A Survey of Theatre Activities in American and Canadian Schools for the Deaf 1965–1970," *American Annals of the Deaf* (June 1974): 339.

9. Gilbert L. Delgado, "A Survey of Sign Language in Junior and Community Colleges," *American Annals of the Deaf* (February 1984): 38.

10. Michael A. Schwartz, "Time for Us to Ask: Whose Theater Is It, Anyway?" *Silent News* (April 1993): 4.

11. Leo Burke, interview with author, February 10, 1989.

EPILOGUE

1993. Thirty-four years later, not only America, but the entire world has experienced dramatic social changes. Gone are the Berlin Wall and the Cold War.

During those years, we experienced the horror of the Vietnam conflict and the success of the Gulf War.

We have become friends with former enemies; enemies with former friends, though most are more tolerant of "differences" than before.

In place of the Studebakers and Hudsons, we now find BMWs and Toyotas. On a good day, you can find a gallon of gasoline for $1.40.

Marilyn, now a legend, has been dead since 1962; Elvis has been commemorated on a stamp.

The Americans with Disabilities Act was signed on July 26, 1990, by President George Bush as thousands of people with disabilities eagerly awaited the social changes they had sought for so long. While its implementation has been slow thus far, progress has been made, and the implications for this legislation are boundless.

We are beginning to see talented people with disabilities portray roles on television and film—positive and productive roles.

Entertainment has taken on altogether new forms—and through it all, NTD has continued her journey.

APPENDIX A

NJD Productions from 1967 to 1995

The following plays are listed chronologically from the first American tour to the 1994–95 season play. Most of the American plays were also presented overseas. Most plays were short pieces that were performed during the fall and spring tours. Some plays were performed by LTD—as indicated and only for the Christmas holiday. Only Saroyan's play was removed after one season, in the fall of 1967.

Touring Season	Play/Author	Description
1967–68	*The Man with His Heart in the Highlands*/William Saroyan	Play
	The Tale of Kasane/Tsuruya Namboku	Poems
	Tyger! Tyger! and Other Burnings/William Blake	Poems
	Gianni Schicchi/Giacomo Puccini	Nonoperatic version
	On the Harmfulness of Tobacco/Anton Chekhov	Play
1968–69	*The Critic*/Richard Sheridan	Play

	The Love of Don Perlimplin and Belisa in the Garden/Federico García Lorca	Play
	Blueprints/Various Authors	Poems
1969–70	*Songs from Milk Wood*/Dylan Thomas	Poem
	Sganarelle/Molière	Play
1970–71	*Woyzeck*/Georg Buchner	Play
	Journeys/Richard Lewis	Poem
1971–72	*My Third Eye*/NTD piece	NTD piece
1972–73	*Gilgamesh*/Based on a Sumerian story	Play
1973–74	*Optimism*/Voltaire	Play
	A Child's Christmas in Wales/Dylan Thomas	Poem (CBS)
1974–75	*The Dybbuk*/Shloime Ansky	Play
	Priscilla, Princess of Power/NTD piece	Play
1975–76	*Parade*/NTD piece	Play
1976–77	*Four Saints in Three Acts*/Virgil Thomson and Gertrude Stein	Opera
	On the Harmfulness of Tobacco/Anton Chekhov	Play
	Children's Letters to God/Eric Marshall and Stuart Hample	Letters
1977–78	*Sir Gawain and the Green Knight*/Dennis Scott	LTD Play
	The Three Musketeers/Alexandre Dumas	NTD piece
	Who Knows One?/NTD piece	TV special
1978–79	*Volpone*/Stefan Zweig	Play
	Quite Early One Morning/Dylan Thomas	Poem
1979–80	*Our Town*/Thornton Wilder	Play
	The Wooden Boy (after Collodi's *Pinocchio*)/David Hays	NTD piece
1980–81	*The Silken Tent*/Robert Frost	TV (poem)
	The Iliad, Play by Play/Shanny Mow (after Homer)	NTD piece

1981–82	*Road to Cordoba*/Federico García Lorca	TV poem
	Issa's Treasure/Issa	Poem
	Gilgamesh/Based on a Sumerian story (Shanny Mow after Larry Arrick)	Play
	The Ghost of Chastity Past, or the Incident at Sashimi Junction/Shanny Mow	NTD piece
1982–83	*Parzival: From the Horse's Mouth*/Shanny Mow and David Hays	NTD piece
1983–84	*The Hero with a Thousand Faces*/Larry Arrick (adapted)	NTD piece
	A Child's Christmas in Wales/Dylan Thomas	Poem
1984–85	*All the Way Home*/Tad Mosel	Play
	A Child's Christmas in Wales/Dylan Thomas	Poem
1985–86	*In a Grove*/Ryunosuke Akutagawa	NTD piece
	Farewell, My Lovely/E. B. White	Poem
	Race a Comet, Catch a Tale/LTD piece	Holiday show
1986–87	*The Heart Is a Lonely Hunter*/Carson McCullers	Novel
	Gift of the Magi/O. Henry	Short story
1987–88	*The Dybbuk: Between Two Worlds*/Shloime Ansky	Play
	A Child's Christmas in Wales/Dylan Thomas/Poem	
1988–89	*The King of Hearts*/NTD piece/Adapted from a movie	
1989–90	*The Odyssey*/Shanny Mow (after Homer)	NTD piece
1990–91	*One More Spring*/J Ranelli	Novel by Robert Nathan

1991–92	*Treasure Island*/Snoo Wilson	Novel by Robert Louis Stevenson
1992–93	*Ophelia*/William Shakespeare (adaptation of *Hamlet*)	NTD piece
1993–94	*Under Milk Wood*/Dylan Thomas	NTD piece
1994–95	*An Italian Straw Hat*/Eugene Labiche and Marc-Michel	Play

APPENDIX B

NTD Alumni List
1967–1993

More than 100 actors, actresses, and stage managers have worked for NTD for periods of time ranging from two months to twenty-six years. The following chart shows the years in which each person worked for NTD.

Alumni	Years with NTD	Additional Information
Carol Addabbo	1979–85	
Carole Aquiline	1978–81	
Violet Armstrong	1967	founding member
Jacqueline Awad	1969–70	
Chuck Baird	1980–87, 1988–90	
John Basinger	1968–70, 1976, 1993–present	
David Berman	1971, 1972	
Adrian Blue	1980, 1982–84, 1986, 1991	
Elena Blue	1983–85, 1986, 1990	
Bob Blumenfeld	1974–76	
Betty Bonni	1975, 1976	
Debbie Bosworth	1981	

Linda Bove	1968–1976, 1978–79	
Bernard Bragg	1967–76	founding member
Candace Broecker	1977–79	
Elaine Bromka	1973, 1974	
Corine Brosket	1968	
Joe Castronovo	1974–75	
Kymberli Colbourne	1990–92	
Janice Cole	1977	
Willy Conley	1987, 1988	
Charles Corey	1967, 1968	founding member
Rita Corey	1977–79	
Robert DeMayo	1990–present	
Colleen Dewhurst		performed with NTD on a television special
Gilbert Eastman	1967	founding member
Sam Edwards	1978	deceased
John Eisner	1987, 1988	
Nanette Fabray		performed with NTD on a television special
Lou Fant	1967–70	founding member
Ed Fearon	1967	founding member
David Fitzsimmons	1978–79, 1983	
Julianna Fjeld	1971–75	
Carol Fleming	1971–72	
Raymond Fleming	1976–77	
Joyce Flynn Lasko	1967	founding member
Phyllis Frelich	1967–1979	founding member
Christopher Grant	1986	
Pat Graybill	1969–77, 1979	
Lily Han	1986	
Charles Hornet	1984, 1985	
Steve Howe	1977	
Dolores Hughes	1984, 1985	
Jessica Hull	1975	
Sandi Inches	1979–1990	
Susan Jackson	1982–85, 1990–92	
Camille Jeter	1987–present	

Tim Johnson	1978, 1979	deceased
Paul Johnston	1975, 1981	
Charles Jones	1976–77	
Karen Josephson	1984	
Michael Josephson	1984	
Richard Kendall	1968–73	
Mark Kindschi	1980	
Troy Kotsur	1991–present	
Jurgen Kuhn	1980	foreign performer invited to tour with NTD
Tetsuko Kuroyanagi	1979, 1986–87	foreign performer invited to tour with NTD
Michael Lamitola	1980–85, 1986–1992, 1993–present	
Lily Lessing	1980	
Alberto Lomnitz	1986	foreign performer invited to tour with NTD
John McRae	1974	foreign performer invited to tour with NTD
Lewis Merkin	1986–88	
Dorothy Miles	1968–72	founding member; deceased
Mary Beth Miller	1968–73	founding member
Shanny Mow	1978–79, 1985–87	
Gene Mirus	1991–present	
Timothy Near	1973, 1974	
Freda Norman	1969–1974, 1976, 1977	
Audree Norton	1967, 1968	founding member
Howard Palmer	1967	founding member
Ray Parks	1976, 1977	
Rico Peterson	1973, 1974, 1977	
Edward Porter	1986–88	
Sir Michael Redgrave		performed with NTD on a television special

Will Rhys	1968–70, 1993–present	founding member
Cathleen Riddley	1986–88	
Chita Rivera		performed with NTD on a television special
Jason Robards		performed with NTD on a television special
Charles Roper	1980–81	
June Russi	1967, 1968	founding member
Jean St. Clair	1980	foreign performer invited to tour with NTD
Joseph Sarpy	1971–77, 1992–present	
Tim Scanlon	1967, 1971–74, 1976, 1979	founding member
Iosif Schneiderman	1990–92	foreign performer invited to tour with NTD
Peggy Schoditsch	1976	
Michael Schwartz	1977	
Howie Seago	1980, 1981	
William Seago	1982, 1983	
Nobauki Sekine	1979, 1988	foreign performer invited to tour with NTD
Dosia Skorobogatov	1978, 1979	foreign performer invited to tour with NTD; deceased
Michael Slipchenko	1975	foreign performer invited to tour with NTD
Lizette Smith	1982, 1983	
Morton Steinberg	1968	founding member
Jody Steiner	1980, 1981	
Meryl Streep		performed with NTD on a television special

Ben Stout	1978, 1979	
Charles Struppmann	1985–91	
Kenneth Swiger	1971, 1972	
Mitutaka Tachinkawa	1981	foreign performer invited to tour with NTD
Izaki Tetsuya	1981, 1982	foreign performer invited to tour with NTD
Marcia Tilchin	1988–90	
Chris Tolliver	1991–present	
James Turner	1976–77	
Andrew Vasnick	1967, 1968, 1980–90	founding member
Joe Velez	1967, 1968	founding member; deceased
Gunilla Wagstrom	1974	foreign performer invited to tour with NTD
Vicki Waltrip	1986	
Ed Waterstreet	1968–75, 1978–79	
Peter Weschberg	1969, 1970	
Ralph White	1967	founding member
Jane Wilk	1969	
Bari Willerford	1982	
Nat Wilson	1979–85, 1988–91	
Sharon Wood	1976	
Akihiro Yonaiyama	1981	foreign performer invited to tour with NTD
Wang Zhen-Tai	1986	foreign performer invited to tour with NTD; deceased

APPENDIX C

Participants in the NTD Deaf Playwrights Conference

Between 1977 and 1982, NTD conducted five deaf playwrights conferences. The participants included a total of five women and nine men. Three of those deaf playwrights participated twice. Since 1978, six playwrights have written works consistently, for a combined total of sixty-five plays as of 1992.

After 1982, the conference was discontinued due to lack of funding and adequate facilities. It has been revived a few times, but the format has been much less intensive.

Year	Playwright	Play
1977	Felix Kowaleski	*Last Supper*
	Arlene Balkauskas	(scene)
	Gregg Brooks	(scene)
	Ruth Brown	(scene)
	Raymond Fleming	(scene)
1978	Steve Baldwin	*Midnight Ride of Billy Dawes*
		A Play of Our Own—Part III
	Ruth Brown	*Safari*
	Shanny Mow	*Daisy and Pole and Billy and Milly and Evelyn and Mike and The Spanking Machine*

1979	Carolyn Ball	*A Start Somewhere*
	Donald Bangs	*Different Worlds*
	Lynn Jacobowitz	*Voyage*
1980	Donald Bangs	*Sea Princess*
	Bruce Hlibok	*Coming Home*
	Maia Nadler	*To Move or Not to Move*
1981	(No DPC)	
1982	Steve Baldwin	*To Quench a Curse*
	Bob Daniels	*Forces Within*
	D. Ray Kennedy	*Go Seek the Blue Jazz Band*

APPENDIX D

Plays by Deaf Playwrights 1955–1993

Below is a list of plays by deaf playwrights. The purpose of this list is to show how the number of plays written by deaf playwrights has increased as NTD has gained in recognition and popularity.

Playwright	Play and Year
Steve Baldwin	*A Play of Our Own—Part III* (1979)
	Borderline (1980)
	Sign and Sound A Lovin' (1980)
	Christmas Oasis (1980)
	A Play of Our Own—Part IV (1981)
	How to Pick a College President (1983)
	Deaf Smith (1985)
	(Baldwin has also written twenty other short plays)
Donald Bangs	*The Touch* (1976)
	Different Worlds (1979)
	Sea Princess (1980)
	The Miser (1981)
	Dracula (1981)
	Jealousy (1985)
	The Phoney (1991)
	Institutional Blues (1993)

Eugene Bergman	*Tales from a Clubroom* (1980)
	Fish nor Fowl (1984)
Adrian Blue	*Circus of Signs* (1982)
Bernard Bragg	*That Makes Two of Us* (1979)
	Tales from a Clubroom (1980)
Douglas Burke	*The Good Peddler* (1961)
Willy Conley	*Broken Spoke* (1990)
	The Hearing Test (1990)
Bob Daniels	*I Didn't Hear the Color* (1990)
	Am I Paranoid? (1992)
Jan Delap	*Institutional Blues* (1993)
Patricia Durr	*Meta* (1993)
Gilbert Eastman	*Sign Me Alice* (1973)
	Hands (1975)
	Laurent Clerc: A Profile (1976)
	What (1981)
	Sign Me Alice II (1983)
	Can Do: A Revue (1989)
Terry Galloway	*2 Women Writers* (1982)
	Out of Their Minds (1984)
	Heart of a Dog (1984)
	Hamlet in Berlin (1985)
	Out All Night and Lost My Shoes (1986)
	Lardo Weeping (1993)
Bruce Hlibok	*Woman Talk* (1984)
	The Deaf Man Howl (1989)
	(Hlibok has also written thirteen other plays)
Tom Holcomb	*Deafasty* (1985)
E. Lynn Jacobowitz	*Deaf History: Time Machine* (1978)
	Deafective (1978)
	Solar System (1978)
	Raggedy Ann and Raggedy Andy (1978)
	Theatre House (1979)
	Voyage (1979)
	Oh, Stop! Oh, Stop! (1981)
Ray Kennedy	*Contract with the Devil* (1981)
	Deafia (1977)
Raymond Luczak	*The Rake* (1992)
Eric Malzkuhn	*Sounds of Silence* (1955)
	Moments Preserved (1966)
Dorothy S. Miles	*A Play of Our Own* (1973)

Shanny Mow	*The Spanking Machine* (1978)
	The Iliad: Play by Play (1980)
	The Ghost of Chastity Past, or Incident at Sashimi Junction (1981)
	Parzival: From the Horse's Mouth (1982)
	The Greatest Little Sign Show on Earth (1988)
	The Odyssey (1989)
	Legend of La Lallorona or the Weeping Woman (1990)
	Letters from Heaven (1991)
	Myths: Baked, Boiled, and Fried (1992)
Terrence J. O'Rourke	*Appointments with Fred* (1989)
Terrylene Theriot-Sacceti	*Molded* (1987)
	Unveiling the Rock (1993)
Howard L. Terry	*The Dream* (1912)
Michele M. Verhoosky	*A Laying of Hands* (1993)
Bruce Weir	*Twenty-five Cents* (1991)

APPENDIX E

NTD Foreign Tours from 1969 to 1992

Touring Season	Country
1969–70	England, France, Israel, Italy, Yugoslavia
1971–72	Denmark, Holland, Israel, Norway, Sweden, Yugoslavia
1972	International Center for Theatre Research—Paris, France
1973–74	Austria, Belgium
1974–75	Australia
1976–77	Australia, Canada, Denmark, New Zealand, Norway, Sweden, Tasmania
1977–78	Portugal
1979–80	Belgium, Denmark, Holland, Japan, Korea, Singapore, West Germany
1980–81	Canada
1981–82	Holland, India, Japan, Liechtenstein, Switzerland, West Germany
1984–85	Germany, Switzerland
1985–86	Hong Kong, India, Nepal, The People's Republic of China
1988	Japan
1992	Northern Ireland, South Africa, Venezuela

Index

Warnings (O'Neill), 9
Waterstreet, Edward, 30, 46, 54, 59–60, 74, 82, 94
Watson, Douglas O., 40
Weitbrecht, Robert, 13–14
Welch, John B., 36
White, E. B., 62
White, George C., 16, 18, 20, 63–64, 114
White, Ralph, 20, 30, 38, 94
Who Knows One, 48
Wilder, Thornton, 14, 47, 104–107
Williams, Boyce R., 11, 17, 114
Wilson, Nat, 91–92

Wilson, Robert, 52
Wold, Sue, 53
Wolf, Peter, 31, 94
The Wooden Boy: The Secret Life of Geppetto's Dummy (Hays), 47, 102
World Games for the Deaf, 65
Woyzeck (Buchner), 47
Wyman, Jane, 53

Yeh, Fanny, 82
Yonaiyama, Akihiro, 69

Zweig, Stefan, 104